MW00639917

From the
Muddy River to the
Ivory Tower

The Journey of
George H. Brimhall

From the
Muddy River to the
Ivory Tower

The Journey of
George H. Brimhall

Mary Jane Woodger
and
Joseph H. Groberg

Foreword by J. Gordon Daines III

BYU Studies
Provo, Utah

Cover and jacket design by Robert E. M. Spencer and Catharine Verhaaren Gruver

Jacket photos: front cover, detail of George H. Brimhall in his 1922 Dodge (courtesy L. Tom Perry Special Collections, Harold B. Lee Library, Brigham Young University); front inside flap, detail of Brimhall in a photo with his sons, ca. 1914 (courtesy Groberg family); back cover (left to right), Brimhall, ca. 1871 (courtesy Groberg family), Brimhall, ca. 1910 (courtesy Perry Special Collections), Brimhall, ca. 1920 (courtesy Perry Special Collections).

Library of Congress Cataloging-in-Publication Data

Woodger, Mary Jane.
    From the Muddy River to the Ivory Tower : The Journey of George H. Brimhall / Mary Jane Woodger and Joseph H. Groberg ; foreword by J. Gordon Daines III.

        p. cm.
    Includes index.
    ISBN 978-0-8425-2765-1 (hard cover : alk. paper)

1. Brimhall, George H. (George Henry), 1852–1932. 2. Brigham Young University—Presidents—Biography. 3. College presidents—United States—Biography. 4. Mormons—United States—Biography. I. Groberg, Joseph H. (Joseph Holbrook), 1942– II. Title.
LD571.B6717W66 2010
378.1'12092—dc22
[B]

2010021871

Printed in the United States of America
10 9 8 7 6 5 4 3 2 1

Dedication

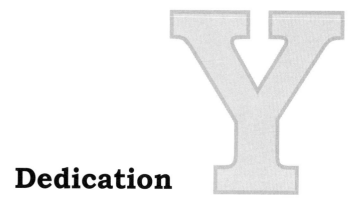

This book is dedicated to Alsina Elisabeth Brimhall Holbrook (1876–1960), the daughter of George H. Brimhall, the mother of eleven children, and the grandmother, great-grandmother, and great–great-grandmother to a posterity numbering approximately one thousand at the date of this printing.

Alsina graduated as valedictorian of her Brigham Young Academy class in 1897. Years later she collected, organized, hand copied, typed, bound, preserved, and, to a limited degree, edited the newspaper articles and other memorabilia about her father, along with his extensive collection of talks, writings, correspondence, and journals. She performed this work anticipating that those materials would be a resource for subsequent generations who might wish to research Brimhall and his university tenure. The volumes Alsina assembled fill an entire bookcase.

When one considers the size and scope of the work she performed—that it was done amidst a busy life of

Alsina Elisabeth Brimhall Holbrook, ca. 1935. Courtesy Groberg family.

service to her family, and before the days of photocopiers and electronic typewriters, let alone scanners and word processors—it becomes an inspiring work of love not only for her father but also for the principles he stood for, which she believed should be passed down to posterity. Although her collection is amazingly complete, there is no question that her personal loyalty to her father and to Church leadership determined what materials to include and emphasize. However, the very tint of those rose-colored glasses gives important insight into what Brimhall taught his children to value.

After many years of working on her father's papers, Alsina was honored by the BYU Alumni Association with the Distinguished Service Award in 1953. In 1966, she (posthumously) and her husband, Lafayette Hinckley Holbrook, were awarded the Joseph F. Smith Family Living Award, also by the alumni association.

Contents

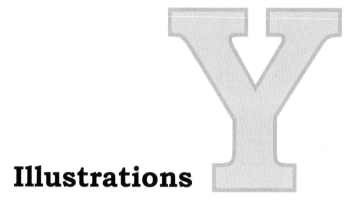

Illustrations

Foreword

In the early twentieth century, a developing tension existed between the sacred and the secular at Brigham Young University (BYU). This tension manifested itself in the differing academic philosophies of Karl G. Maeser, who established the spiritual architecture, and Benjamin Cluff Jr., who established the academic architecture of the university. This juxtaposition sets the stage for understanding the life of George H. Brimhall and his work at BYU. As one of the early leaders of that institution, he played an important role in solidifying the university's mission to integrate academic excellence with spiritual development.

One of the remarkable features of BYU is its attempt to integrate academic excellence with spiritual development. This integration of the sacred and the secular is unique in an American academic environment where "the free exercise of religion does not extend to the dominant intellectual centers of our culture."[1] This uniqueness has its roots in the establishment of the university as Brigham Young Academy in 1875 by Brigham Young, then president of The Church of Jesus Christ of Latter-day Saints.

Young had long considered education to be vital to the well-being of the Saints. This belief in education was dramatically underscored by advice he gave to Church members as they were being driven from their homes in Illinois. He encouraged them to obtain

> a copy of every valuable treatise on education—every book, map, chart, or diagram that may contain interesting, useful, and attractive matter, to gain the attention of children, and cause them to love to learn to read; and, also every historical, mathematical, scientific, practical, and all other variety of useful and interesting writings, maps, &c., to present to the General Church Recorder, when they shall arrive at their destination, from which important and interesting matter may be gleaned to compile the most valuable works, on every science and subject, for the benefit of the rising generation.[2]

This material was to be used in the educational institutions that the Latter-day Saints hoped to establish wherever they happened to end up.

Once in Utah Territory, Church leaders revived their educational endeavors with the establishment of "common schools, stake academies, and colleges and universities."[3] Young began to consider the possibility of establishing an institution of higher education in his name in the early 1870s.[4] The development of this idea is well documented in correspondence with Thomas L. Kane.[5] In late 1873, Kane wrote,

> The most cheery, probably the most important feature of the tidings brought by Mr. Cannon is your

resolve to found an Educational Institution worthy to bear your name. It is impossible to deprecate too seriously the growing practice of sending your bright youths abroad to lay the basis of the opinions of their lives on the crumbling foundations of modern unfaith and specialism. Why should you not inaugurate a system of education informed upon by your own experience of the world, embodying your own dearly earned wisdom, and calculated peradventure to endure for ages with the stamp of your originality upon it?

Kane continued by highlighting what he saw as the benefits of establishing a university under direct Church control. He advised Young that

the young fledglings who would resort to our Eastern seminaries of learning—to learn what you will hardly be able to unteach them all their days—should even now be training in the Brigham Young University, a Normal College of the highest grade, to officiate as "Zion" tutors and professors.[6]

Young already had his eye on a potential school in Utah County. In 1870 the University of Deseret had established a branch campus in Provo called the Timpanogos Branch of the University of Deseret. The school was directed by Warren N. Dusenberry and was quite popular. It was housed in the Lewis Building, which was owned by Young.[7]

In 1875 when the Timpanogos Branch was in danger of closing because of the financial difficulties of its parent institution, Young stepped in and took over the school. The doors of the Timpanogos Branch closed and the next day the school reopened as the Brigham Young Academy (BYA). Young had a specific vision of what he hoped the school would be able to accomplish. The deed of trust establishing the academy states,

> The beneficiaries of this Academy shall be members in good standing in the Church of Jesus Christ of Latter-day Saints, or shall be the children of such members, and each of the boys who shall take a full course, if his physical ability will permit, shall be taught some branch of mechanism that shall be suitable to his taste and capacity; and all pupils shall be instructed in reading, penmanship, orthography, grammar[,] geography and mathematics, together with such other branches as are usually taught in an academy of learning; and the Old and New Testaments, the Book of Mormon and the Book of Doctrine and Covenants shall be read and their doctrines inculcated in the Academy.[8]

In executing a deed that specified that secular learning be integrated with sacred learning, Young laid the groundwork for the grand experiment that is today's Brigham Young University. The role of the sacred in relation to the secular was further augmented in the instructions Young gave to Karl G. Maeser, the institution's first full-time principal. Young told Maeser that "neither the alphabet nor the multiplication table were to be taught without the Spirit of God."[9] Both Young and Maeser understood this to mean that the sacred and the secular would intermingle in the new institution.

In his book *School and Fireside*, Maeser elaborated on the unique character of the fledgling BYA. He wrote,

> With a view to counteract the tendency of modern education toward infidelity, President Brigham Young did all in his power to introduce a system of training that should include the principles of the Gospel, the

germ of which system was planted in the founding of the Brigham Young Academy.[10]

Maeser further underscored the importance of integrating the sacred and the secular in an address he gave at the academy's first Founder's Day. He explained,

> There must go through it all, like a golden thread, one thing constant: the spirit of the latter-day work. As long as this principle shall be the mainspring of all her labors, whether in teaching the alphabet or the multiplication tables, or unfolding the advanced truths of science and art, the future of Brigham Young Academy will surpass in glory the fondest hopes of her most ardent admirers.[11]

Maeser understood that the uniqueness of Young's charge lay in the integration of the sacred and the secular. To ensure the sacred influenced all that occurred at the academy, Maeser "placed the development of character above the development of intellect."[12] Daily devotionals became an important part of academy life, and the Domestic Organization[13] was established to help students make appropriate choices when they were not in school. Maeser's emphasis on the sacred laid an important spiritual foundation that continues to influence the university in the early twenty-first century.

One of the students attracted to BYA by Maeser was Benjamin Cluff Jr. One of Cluff's uncles, Harvey H. Cluff, took young Benjamin to the academy following his arrival in Provo and introduced him to Principal Maeser. Maeser made young Cluff feel welcome, and he became a student at BYA in spring 1877.[14] Cluff was destined to have a significant impact on the institution and its efforts to integrate the sacred and the secular.

Cluff excelled in his studies at BYA and distinguished himself as a student in the Normal school.[15] That Cluff was offered an instructorship in the Primary Department toward the end of fall term 1877 provides evidence of his exceptional abilities as a teacher. The Primary Department was responsible for educating the students enrolled in the first eight grades of common school—what we now know as elementary school and middle school. Cluff taught in the Primary Department until late 1878, when he was called to serve a mission in the Sandwich Islands. His mission lasted until 1882. Upon completion of a successful mission, Cluff returned to Provo and resumed his teaching duties in the Primary Department. He taught there until 1886, when he took a leave of absence to obtain further education at the University of Michigan.[16]

At the University of Michigan, Benjamin Cluff distinguished himself as a scholar and polished his skills as a writer by defending doctrines of The Church of Jesus Christ of Latter-day Saints in print. He earned a Bachelor of Science degree in 1890 and, at the urging of his professors, made arrangements to work on a master's degree. Cluff did the majority of his work toward this degree in Provo, with a period of time spent at the University of Michigan. He was awarded his master's degree in 1894. While at the University of Michigan, Cluff formed a close friendship with James Burrill Angell, then president of the University of Michigan. Cluff was deeply influenced by Angell's views of education. Angell once told Cluff that "we make universities out of men and not out of bricks and mortar." At Michigan, Cluff was exposed to the works of several of the most influential educators of his time. Among these men were Charles W. Eliot, John Dewey, and Aaron B. Hinsdale.[17]

Upon returning to his teaching post at BYA in 1891, Cluff became embroiled in controversy with Karl Maeser. Maeser was extremely wary of Eastern education. He felt too many students who studied in the East lost their religious faith in the course of their studies. He also felt it was inappropriate for faculty educated in the East to teach at BYA because their lack of faith would be detrimental to the impressionable students attending the academy.[18] Consequently, Maeser "feared that Cluff would introduce unwelcome changes in the school."[19] This controversy was eventually resolved with an uneasy truce that left Cluff as Maeser's assistant principal.

In 1892, however, Cluff became principal of BYA and began introducing many of the changes that Maeser had feared. Cluff strongly felt the educational stature of the academy needed to be strengthened and began to do this by improving the caliber of the faculty. In a letter to George H. Brimhall, written in 1893 while Cluff was at the University of Michigan fulfilling requirements for his master's degree, Cluff stated

> news reaches me that a movement is a foot to unite in some way the Church University with the U. of Utah by establishing a theological chair close to the latter. Should this be done, I am certain emphasis will be given to the Academy and it will immediately increase in importance. We want, therefore, the most modern methods and the best trained teachers we can get.[20]

He encouraged many of the existing faculty to further their education by studying back east and was successful in recruiting new faculty to the academy. Cluff believed the key to successful recruitment of new faculty members was to give them the opportunity to improve their teaching skills. He wrote to Brimhall, explaining

> that every encouragement should be given the professors to work up in their branches and work up

their branches, and it shall be my policy as principal so long as I may be honored with that title, to encourage teachers to study, and furnish means for study, and I might say that positions in the Academy should depend on merit.[21]

Many of the new faculty members attracted to the academy were students who Cluff had encouraged to go east for education at the University of Michigan, Michigan State College, and Harvard. BYA's faculty grew from fourteen in 1890 to sixty in 1903.[22]

As part of his effort to improve the educational experience for students, Cluff brought prominent educators to campus as guest lecturers. He strengthened the academy's curriculum and began the first steps toward becoming a university with the establishment of the Collegiate Department. Cluff lengthened class periods and increased the time required to train teachers from two years to six. He also successfully lobbied for the Board of Trustees to change the name of the academy to Brigham Young University and became the new university's first president.[23]

Cluff believed that BYA needed to be an exceptional academic institution, and he worked very hard to successfully create a strong educational architecture for the academy. Because his tenure emphasized academic excellence, this created natural tensions with individuals who believed that what made BYA unique was its emphasis on the sacred.

When Brimhall became the second president of BYU in 1904, he inherited an institution still struggling to find a balance between its two identities. These tensions came to a head with the Modernism crisis of 1911. Brimhall was forced to confront a difficult dilemma as a result of this crisis. Should BYU strive for academic excellence, as advocated by Brimhall's friend and predecessor Benjamin Cluff? Or should

BYU focus on the spiritual, as Brimhall's mentor and teacher Karl G. Maeser had insisted? Or was it possible to do both—and to do them well? This book tells the story of George H. Brimhall and how he helped the university begin to reconcile the tension between the sacred and the secular. It gives readers a glimpse into the life of the man who made it possible for BYU to become accredited under Franklin S. Harris and who helped demonstrate that the secular can be integrated with the sacred in meaningful ways.

J. Gordon Daines III
University Archivist
Brigham Young University

Notes

1. George M. Marsden, *The Soul of the American University: From Protestant Establishment to Established Nonbelief* (New York: Oxford University Press, 1994), 6.

2. James R. Clark, comp., *Messages of the First Presidency of The Church of Jesus Christ of Latter-day Saints, 1833–1964* (Salt Lake City: Bookcraft, 1965), 1:331.

3. Thomas G. Alexander, *Mormonism in Transition: A History of the Latter-day Saints, 1890–1930* (Urbana: University of Illinois Press, 1996), 157.

4. Ernest L. Wilkinson, ed., *Brigham Young University: The First One Hundred Years,* 4 vols. (Provo, Utah: Brigham Young University Press, 1975), 1:62.

5. Thomas L. Kane was a prominent politician, Civil War general, abolitionist, and philanthropist who befriended the Latter-day Saints and carried on a prolific correspondence with Brigham Young. For more on this relationship with the Saints, see David J. Whittaker, ed., *Colonel Thomas L. Kane and the Mormons, 1847–1883* (Provo, Utah, and Salt Lake City: Brigham Young University Press and University of Utah Press, 2010).

6. Photocopy of a letter from Thomas L. Kane to Brigham Young, December 4, 1873, in UA 566, Centennial History Committee records, University Archives, L. Tom Perry Special Collections, Harold B. Lee Library, Brigham Young University, Provo, Utah (hereafter cited as Perry Special Collections).

7. Wilkinson, *First One Hundred Years,* 1:51–53. For more information about the Dusenberrys and the Timpanogos Branch of the University of Deseret see Wilkinson, *First One Hundred Years,* 1:31–49.

8. Handwritten copy of the deed of trust, October 16, 1875, UA 6, Brigham Young University Board of Trustees records, 1875–1985, University Archives, Perry Special Collections, 1–3.

9. Dedicatory exercises of the Brigham Young Academy Building, 1892, UA SC 33, University Archives, Perry Special Collections, 2.

10. Karl G. Maeser, *School and Fireside* (Provo, Utah: Skelton, 1898), 168.

11. Karl G. Maeser, "History of the Academy," in *Educating Zion,* ed. John W. Welch and Don E. Norton (Provo, Utah: BYU Studies, 1996), 4.

12. Wilkinson, *First One Hundred Years,* 1:207.

13. The Domestic Organization as organized by Karl G. Maeser was designed to ensure that students behaved appropriately when they were not in school. Among the responsibilities assigned to the Domestic Organization were the approval of student housing and implementation of the Visitorial System. The Visitorial System allowed the administration to keep a close watch on the "manners, morals and activities of the Academy students." Students were assigned by the school to visit their classmates every couple of weeks to determine if they were following school regulations. For more information on the Domestic Organization and the Visitorial System see Wilkinson, *First One Hundred Years,* 1:199–201.

14. Eugene L. Roberts and Mrs. Eldon Reed Cluff, *Benjamin Cluff Jr.: Scholar, Educational Administrator, and Explorer, Second Principal of Brigham Young Academy, and First President of Brigham Young University: A study of the Life and Labors of One of Utah's First School Administrators* (Provo, Utah: 1947), 14.

15. The Normal school was the teacher education component of BYA.

16. For more information on Cluff's early years at Brigham Young Academy and his mission to Hawaii see Roberts and Cluff, *Benjamin Cluff Jr.*, 16–31, and Wilkinson, *First One Hundred Years,* 1:213–214.

17. For more information on Cluff's experience at the University of Michigan see Roberts and Cluff, *Benjamin Cluff Jr.,* 32–52 and Wilkinson, *First One Hundred Years,* 1:214–15.

18. Wilkinson, *First One Hundred Years,* 1:215–216.

19. Wilkinson, *First One Hundred Years,* 1:216.

20. Benjamin Cluff Jr. to George H. Brimhall, November 12, 1893, UA 1093, Benjamin Cluff Jr. Presidential Records, 1892–1904, University Archives, Perry Special Collections.

21. Benjamin Cluff Jr. to George H. Brimhall, November 12, 1893, UA 1093, Cluff Presidential Records, University Archives, Perry Special Collections; underlining in original.

22. Wilkinson, *First One Hundred Years,* 1:259.

23. For more information on Cluff's achievements in strengthening the educational architecture of BYA see Wilkinson, *First One Hundred Years,* 1:375–81.

Preface

George H. Brimhall was born in frontier Utah five years after the arrival of the first Mormon pioneers. It was a rough physical environment in which scarcity and poverty were the rule, but it was a rich spiritual and intellectual environment. Very early in life, Brimhall realized that faith in and loyalty to The Church of Jesus Christ of Latter-day Saints had been the guiding force in his family. He adopted education as the means through which he could best serve that cause.

Brimhall loved schools and teaching. He believed the advancement of knowledge was the advancement of truth and, therefore, the advancement of his faith. However, when conflicts developed, his loyalties did not change. Some of the notable individuals with whom Brimhall was closely associated and to whom he remained loyal throughout his life include Wilson and Warren Dusenberry, the founders of what later became Brigham Young University (BYU); Karl G. Maeser, appointed by Brigham Young as successor to the Dusenberrys; Benjamin Cluff Jr., the first president of the university; Jesse Knight, the school's early, critical benefactor; three generations of Abraham Smoots, key local supporters of BYU; Franklin S. Harris, Brimhall's pupil and successor; Wilford Woodruff, Lorenzo Snow, Joseph F. Smith, and Heber J. Grant, as presidents of the Church; Reed Smoot, James E. Talmage, John A. Widtsoe, George Albert Smith, and David O. McKay, leaders in Church education; and Joseph B. Keeler, Edwin S. Hinckley, and Amos N. Merrill, Brimhall's counselors in the university presidency. These people are but a few of the many with whom Brimhall developed and maintained close personal friendships, which, in turn, enabled him to carry out his life's work.

We gratefully acknowledge the help of the L. Tom Perry Special Collections staff of BYU's Harold B. Lee Library; the efforts of Alsina Elisabeth Brimhall Holbrook, to whom this book is dedicated, and her daughter Jennie Holbrook Groberg in organizing and preserving Brimhall's talks and writings; Raymond and Esther Holbrook for publishing *The Tall Pine Tree*, an early biography of Brimhall; Mary Jane Fritzen, Brimhall's great granddaughter, who pulled everything together for this book after Joseph H. Groberg was called on a Church mission; John W. Welch and Heather M. Seferovich of BYU Studies for patiently and helpfully overseeing the entire process and for bringing into that process Josh Probert and Caitlin Shirts, who gave invaluable research assistance; Catharine Verhaaren Gruver for design and layout and Marny K. Parkin for production and indexing; Andrea Howard, Audrey Paurus, and Elizabeth Pew for their assistance with source checking and copyediting; John H. and Richard H. Groberg, trustees of the D. V. and Jennie H. Groberg Family Trust, for reviewing key portions of the book and for supporting its publication; and to John Holbrook, Lyle Anderson, Carol Maxwell Christiansen,

Nora Mae Brown Brown, Louine Berry Hunter Skankey, Kathleen Dahlquist Crapo, Rebecca Heninger Jewkes, and David Haymore for reading through many of the volumes of Brimhall's writings to identify materials to be included in this biography.

George H. Brimhall Chronology

December 9, 1852	Born in Salt Lake City to George Washington Brimhall and Rachel Ann Mayer.
1854	Moved with family to Ogden, where he later began schooling.
March 1864 or 1865	Started for the Muddy River Mission with parents and five siblings.
1865 (or 1866)	Returned with family to Spanish Fork.
1865–1870	Lived in Spanish Fork, oldest of ten children.
1870	Assisted in teaching at a Spanish Fork school.
April 1870	Dusenberry school in Provo became the Timpanogos Campus of the University of Deseret.

1871	Attended Dusenberry's Timpanogos University.
October 1872	Helped build Young Men's Academy in Spanish Fork.
1874	Attended Dusenberry's Timpanogos University and taught in the Young Men's Academy.
December 28, 1874	Married Alsina E. Wilkins in Endowment House, Salt Lake City.
April 1875	Dusenberry school (Timpanogos campus of University of Deseret) closed.
June 10, 1875	Young Men's Mutual Improvement Association (YMMIA) organized.
October 16, 1875	Dusenberry's Timpanogos Branch of the University of Deseret reopened as Brigham Young Academy (BYA).
November 20, 1875	Granted teacher's certificate by Utah County Board of Examination.
December 13, 1875	Alsina's first child, Lucy Jane (Jennie), was born in Spanish Fork.
April 15, 1876	Warren Dusenberry resigned as principal of BYA and Karl G. Maeser was named principal.
April 24, 1876	Included among students at BYA at end of BYA's first term.
December 16, 1876	Alsina's second child, Alsina Elisabeth (Sina), was born in Spanish Fork.
1877	Received Normal diploma from BYA and became principal teacher (with additional administrative responsibilities) in Spanish Fork elementary school.

October 25, 1878	Alsina's third child, George Washington, was born in Spanish Fork.
June 18, 1880	Alsina's fourth child, Mark, was born in Spanish Fork.
April 26, 1882	Alsina's fifth child, Wells, was born in Spanish Fork.
1883	Elected Superintendent of Utah County schools. Called as counselor to Benjamin Cluff Jr. in Utah Stake YMMIA superintendency.
October 21, 1883	Alsina's sixth child, Milton Albert, was born in Spanish Fork.
October & November 1883	Wife, Alsina, became ill.
January 8, 1884	Son Milton Albert died.
1885	Named to five-man committee to write lessons for YMMIA curriculum.
September 11, 1885	Married Flora Robertson in Logan Temple.
November 14, 1885	Alsina was institutionalized in a mental care facility in Provo.
December 11, 1886	Flora's first child, Dean Robertson, was born in Provo.
January 15, 1887	Called to be superintedent of the Utah Stake YMMIA. Benjamin Cluff Jr. left for school in Michigan.
1888	Named Superintendent of Provo City schools and moved family to Provo.
March 20, 1889	Went before a U.S. Commissioner on charges of polygamy.
April 20, 1889	Received suspended sentence for polygamy.

May 16, 1889	Flora's second and third children, twin girls Fawn and Fay, were born in Spanish Fork.
January 16, 1891	Licensed by Church General Board of Education to teach in the Provo Ward.
April 15, 1891	Licensed by the Church General Board of Education to teach intermediate grades at any Church school.
1891	Invited to join teaching staff at BYA.
January 19, 1892	Flora's fourth child, Burns Robertson, was born in Salt Lake City.
Fall 1893–Spring 1894	Served as acting principal of BYA while Benjamin Cluff Jr. was in Michigan working on a master's degree.
April 8, 1895	Flora's fifth child, Ruth Afton, was born in Provo.
July–August 1897	Served proselyting mission to Colorado.
1897, 1898	Elected president of Utah Education Association.
April 1, 1898	First child, Jennie, was called to serve a proselyting mission in Great Britain. She and her companion, Inez Knight, are generally considered the first single female missionaries for the Church.
June 9, 1898	Flora's sixth child, Paul Robertson, was born in Provo.
November 18, 1898	Received a Doctor in Science and Didactics degree from the General Church Board of Education.
January 18, 1899	First child, Jennie, married Jesse William (Will) Knight.

1900	Introduced parenting classes for all adults in Provo area.
April 1900	Named acting president of BYA when Benjamin Cluff Jr. left on a scientific expedition to South America.
February 16, 1901	Spoke at the funeral of Karl G. Maeser.
April 1, 1901	BYA Board of Trustees was reorganized with Joseph F. Smith as president.
May 14, 1901	Asked BYA's board of trustees for a training school building.
May 15, 1901	Second child, Sina, married Lafayette Hinckley Holbrook.
June 25, 1901	Church leaders decided to keep the college division of BYA rather than consolidate all college work at the University of Utah.
July 23, 1901	Flora's seventh child, Alta, was born in Provo.
October 17, 1901	Joseph F. Smith became President of the Church.
February 7, 1902	Benjamin Cluff Jr. returned from his expedition.
March 1902	Became very ill.
April 22, 1902	Traveled to California to recover health.
April 25, 1903	Alta, one-year-old daughter, was accidentally killed. Returned to Provo.
July 1903	Traveled to Canada.
October 1903	Brigham Young Academy became Brigham Young University.

November 17, 1903	Benjamin Cluff Jr. resigned as president of BYU.
December 1903	Received letter from Joseph F. Smith asking him to be acting president of BYU.
April 16, 1904	Inaugurated as president of BYU.
1904	BYU authorized to confer Bachelor of Science degrees.
1904–1908	Upper Campus was purchased.
1906	Block Y was built on Y Mountain. Bachelor of Arts degree replaced Bachelor of Pedagogy degree at BYU.
August 12, 1906	Flora's eighth child, Golden Henry, was born in Provo.
1907	Developed plans for the construction of the Maeser Memorial. Joseph and Henry Peterson were hired at BYU.
July 7, 1907	Crossed the same territory by train that he traveled as a boy to the Muddy Mission.
January 16, 1908	Site for Maeser Memorial dedicated.
1908	Ralph Chamberlin was hired at BYU.
February 1909	Church Board of Education confirmed BYU as the Church's official teachers college.
August 3, 1909	Flora's ninth child, Areo Robertson, was born in Provo.
1909	Joseph F. Smith laid the cornerstone of the Maeser Memorial.
November & December 1910	Horace Cummings, Superintendent of Church Schools, visited BYU to check on alleged unorthodox teachings.

February–March 1911	Joseph Peterson, Henry Peterson, and Ralph Chamberlin were asked by the Church Board of Education to change their curriculums.
March 13, 1911	Students rallied in opposition to ultimatum given to their professors.
Fall 1911	Maeser Memorial was completed.
May 30, 1912	Maeser Memorial was dedicated.
1913	Women's Gymnasium was built.
1915	Edwin S. Hinckley was released as counselor. Amos N. Merrill was named in his place.
1917	Began writing lessons for Advanced Senior Class of the YLMIA.
April 1917	America entered the First World War.
July 3, 1918	BYU assets were transferred to the Church. Church assumed liabilities of BYU.
1918	Mechanic Arts Building was built on upper campus.
October 1918	Army Training Corps program commenced.
November 23, 1918	Heber J. Grant became president of the Church.
1919	Church Board of Education approved Masters of Arts degrees for BYU.
July 20, 1919	Asked to supervise the seminary program of the Church and to appoint a faculty executive committee to help administer BYU.

April 26, 1921	Church Board of Education announced Brimhall's release as president of BYU.
June 27, 1921	Conferred an honorary doctorate degree by the Church Board of Education.
July 1, 1921	Officially released as president of BYU and made President Emeritus. Placed in charge of department of Theology at BYU and of Church seminaries.
November 1921	Began writing lessons for the *Relief Society Magazine*.
January 10, 1926	First wife, Alsina, was brought home from the mental hospital and died the same day.
1929	Gave talks for the Mutual Improvement Association over the radio.
1932	Wrote his last articles for the *Improvement Era*.
July 29, 1932	Died at home in Provo.
October 16, 1935	George H. Brimhall building on BYU campus was dedicated by Heber J. Grant.
May 1, 1950	Flora Robertson Brimhall died in Salt Lake City.

"We are more as a family than we would have been had father and mother never been called to The Muddy Mission and filled it to the satisfaction of the leaders of the Church."

George H. Brimhall, 1907

1

Youth in Pioneer Utah

George Henry Brimhall grew up in pioneer Utah. His childhood was filled with hard labor necessary for survival. His family zigzagged across Utah as his father was called to colonizing missions throughout the territory. Despite the rough conditions of the frontier and the frequent moves, however, his parents always encouraged him to attend school, which he loved. These three things from his childhood—the intense labor and hardship of frontier life, his parents' willingness to do what the leaders of The Church of Jesus Christ of Latter-day Saints asked them to do, and his enchantment with education—combined to powerfully shape his character.

George W. Brimhall and the Iron Mission

George H.'s father, George Washington Brimhall, a native of Oneida, New York,[1] joined the Church in September 1832 at age eighteen. Eighteen years later, he left Nauvoo, Illinois, to join the Saints in the Rocky Mountains. However, his wife, Lucretia Metcalfe, refused to leave Nauvoo.[2] There is no evidence that she ever joined the Church, and, according to report, she felt that "going to the Rocky Mountains was too hard." The two parted ways, never to see each other again. She kept their three children and in 1857 obtained a divorce.[3] In fact, life was difficult in pioneer Utah, and it was especially difficult in southern Utah, where George W. lived during three separate colonizing missions.

The first mission for George W. was the Iron Mission. After receiving reports of significant deposits of iron ore in the southern part of the territory and of coal in the Little Muddy Creek, Church President Brigham Young dispatched more than a hundred men to settle in what later became Iron County. George W. Brimhall was included in this company. Under the direction of George A. Smith, George W. was called to help build a fort at Parowan. While working in the Iron Mission, George W. also recorded that his "office was that of road commissioner and prosecuting attorney." Additionally, Iron County records list him as a millwright.[4] In 1851 he was selected to represent Iron County in the Utah Territorial legislature.[5]

While attending the 1852 session of the territorial legislature, George W. met President Young on the streets of Salt Lake City. Young inquired about George W. being single, to which he related his painful parting from his wife in Nauvoo. Young counseled George W. to marry and make a home with a new wife in southern Utah. Soon thereafter, he met Rachel Ann Mayer.[6] Rachel was born February 9, 1829, in Crawford County, Ohio, the oldest of eight children. Her father joined the Church on November 11, 1843, with the rest of the family soon following. At age nineteen, she drove a team of oxen west to Utah.[7] To help with family finances, she found employment as a housekeeper in the home where George W. stayed during the legislative session. George W. proposed,

George Washington Brimhall, ca. 1885. Courtesy Groberg family.

Rachel accepted, and President Young performed the marriage in the Council House on February 2, 1852, less than
a month after the legislative session had begun. The couple
"left for Iron County immediately, thereafter."[8]

Back in Iron County, George W. studied law under
Zerubbabel Snow, judge of the Third Judicial District, "and
was admitted to the bar to practice [law] in the United States
courts in the Territory of Utah."[9] Snow was an associate
justice of the Utah Supreme Court, and he later became
the attorney general, who resided in Salt Lake, but he

held court in Parowan, Iron County, at least once a year. It seems George W. was able to study under Snow in southern Utah and possibly later in Salt Lake as well.[10] Eventually, the Brimhall family moved back to Salt Lake City, where their first son was born on December 9, 1852. George W. recorded: "Here we had a son born to us, a puny little boy, who with care began to grow. We called his name George Henry."[11]

About a year later the family moved to Ogden to help establish Junction City because George W. became weary of the legal world. He later recalled, "The intricacies of law were more difficult to follow than the trail of an Indian over the glaciers of ice or the flat smooth rocks of the mountains."[12] In Ogden, the Brimhalls were caught up in the heat of the Utah War.

In addition to the normal agricultural pursuits of a small farm and livestock, George W. organized a literary society and opened "a free school" at the request of the Ogden City

George Henry's birthplace, Salt Lake City, ca. 1920. Courtesy Groberg family.

mayor and also served as a member of the city council. Protecting the youth from the influences of the army had been a primary reason for creating the school, but it was not successful. It was in Odgen at age seven that George Henry attended his first formal school.[13] George W. moved his family back to Salt Lake City in 1863.[14]

Exploring the Virgin River Area

In 1852 explorers dispatched by Brigham Young traveled to the red rock deserts of southern Utah and reported that the climate was ideal for growing cotton, grapes, tobacco, sugar cane, and other crops that would contribute to the self-sufficiency of the Latter-day Saints. Soon after, Young sent hundreds of settlers to southern Utah to establish a Cotton Mission in what became known as southern Utah's Dixie.

George W.'s family was among those called in the early 1860s "to go south ... to encourage the people and strengthen the settlements on the Rio Virgin River."[15] The family settled in Grafton, in Kane County, on the Virgin River east of St. George, where George W. worked surveying land throughout the area.[16]

George W. developed a close relationship with his oldest son, George H. The father recalled,

> I now found a true friend in my son, George Henry, a little wiry willing lad, with quick perceptive views, good memory and original thought. We soon began operations, climbing the mountains, bringing down cedars for fencing, clearing off land for wheat, sowing and working on water ditches for irrigation.[17]

He wrote that George H. was "almost my constant attendant, a brilliant light, in my view, a coming star in the grand galaxy of the wise, and a sublime terror to ignorance, the worst enemy of man."[18]

After exploring in the Virgin River area of southern Utah, George W. made arrangements to return north for supplies. He wrote:

> I sold my house for two bales of cotton and an odd ox, and donated one bale to build a meetinghouse at St. George. We were soon on our way to the upper country for supplies, expecting to return as soon as we could, but while at Spanish Fork, the committee of safety sent one of their number, George A. Smith, to ask me to go south again and explore, to learn if there were any good places for settlement on the Colorado River.[19]

The call came as a surprise to George W. He wrote, "I had never refused a mission from the committee as yet, and did not wish to this time, although I did not like it."[20] His reservations were not without merit as the terrain surrounding this region of the Colorado River was even more severe than what he had explored in the Virgin River area. George W. had worked and lived among those in the Cotton Mission of Dixie and other settlements and knew how immensely trying life was in the blazing heat. He later wrote of the new area he was asked to explore and, if possible, help settle, part of which became the Muddy Mission:

> To describe this country and its sterility for one hundred miles, its gloomy barrenness, would subject the reader's credulity to too high a strain. Not even the caw of a crow, or the bark of a wolf, was there to break the awful monotony. I could see something green on the tops of the distant mountains, a thousand feet above me, but here there was nothing but a continual stench of miasma, and hot streaks of poisonous air to breathe. Was this Hades, sheole, or

the place for the condign punishment of the wicked? or was it the grand sewer for the waste and filth of vast animation?[21]

George W. sought strength and direction from deity in making the move. He received an answer to his prayer that was fraught with the reality of the sacrifice his discipleship would require. He recalled, "I sought Him for information, and was told that I might go, but it would be the destruction of about all of my hard earned property." Stepping back from such a stark prophetic answer to prayer, George W. lacked the desire to go. So he prayed again, this time asking God to give him the desire. "He did," George W. matter-of-factly recorded, "and I began to make ready."[22]

The Muddy Mission

The desire to establish a Mormon colony on the Muddy River and the prospect of settlements even further south were multifaceted. Historian Audrey Godfrey detailed three principal reasons. First, Brigham Young wanted a continuous corridor of Mormon settlements running from the Colorado River to Salt Lake City. The connection to the Colorado River would allow for the shipping of goods and for the transportation of immigrating Latter-day Saints from the Gulf of California. Second, Young wanted cotton to be grown along the Muddy River to supply the Church's factory in Washington, near St. George. And third, Young saw non-Mormon, or Gentile, control of the area as a threat, so he wanted Mormons to occupy the lands first.[23]

George W. and his family began their journey to the Muddy Mission in early 1865.[24] His son George H. was only twelve years old and had to take on great responsibilities for the family. With his wagon, two yokes of oxen, two milk cows, and six children,[25] George W. headed south again. They were

The Iron, Cotton, and Muddy Missions

After arriving in Utah, the Saints exerted their efforts into developing the local resources, establishing missions to develop and cultivate iron, cotton, sugar, lead, silk, wool, flax, and even wine and tobacco.

The Iron Mission, which began in 1851, brought settlers to present-day Parowan and Cedar City. Although this area was rich in iron ore, the Saints faced many difficulties in refining it, such as floods, crop failures, technical problems, and insufficient financing. Despite the missionaries' determination, attempts at an iron industry ended in 1858.

As the misfortunes of the Iron Mission grew, the Saints undertook a new venture. In 1857 a small group of settlers went to the Virgin and Santa Clara River basins to grow cotton and other semitropical crops. When this early group met some success, the Cotton Mission formally began in 1861. In time, the new settlements, including St. George, had more success with grapes and molasses than cotton.

In 1864, another pioneering mission began—the Muddy Mission. This effort was more ill fated than the other two. The settlers to the Muddy were also instructed to grow cotton, but the area's severe climate made that task very difficult. Although they were able to raise some cotton, the settlers' efforts were thwarted by extreme temperatures, insect infestation, floods, disease, and fire. In 1870 a survey discovered that the mission was actually in Nevada, not Utah, and Brigham Young instructed the nearly destitute settlers to return to Utah Territory. When the Boulder Dam (now the Hoover Dam) was built in the 1930s, much of the Muddy Mission disappeared under Lake Mead.

Arrington, Leonard J. "Religion and Economics in Mormon History." *BYU Studies* 3, no. 3 (1961): 15–33.

Arrington, Leonard J. *Great Basin Kingdom: An Economic History of the Latter-day Saints, 1830–1900.* Cambridge, Mass.: Harvard University Press, 1958.

Shirts, Morris A., and Kathryn H. Shirts. *A Trial Furnace: Southern Utah's Iron Mission.* Provo, Utah: Brigham Young University Press, 2001.

sent farther south by Church leader Erastus Snow to meet Thomas S. Smith, leader of the St. Thomas colony. After meeting Smith, the Brimhall family traveled even further to establish a colony on the Muddy River, about 125 miles west of St. George. George W. described the trek:

> The road extended up the river bed about seven miles. On either side the banks were abrupt and rocky so that we could not get out with our wagons. It was slow pulling against such a stream. The women ... went ashore, footing it on the side of the mountain, over rocks, gulches, [and] precipitous ravines. . . . The bottom was continually moving sand and pebbles, which filled our shoes full of rocks, making our feet very tender. . . . On taking off my shoes, the sand and gravel had worn the bottom of my feet entirely out.[26]

Reaching the settlement of St. Thomas,[27] George W. recalled, "I looked at the country and thought if I found nothing better I should return, but I must see [the] Colorado first."[28] Thomas S. Smith offered the Brimhalls the services of an Indian guide to accompany them on their trip to the Colorado River—a trip that almost cost them their lives. Their oxen became ill after drinking from a stream of water. They "were lying on the ground, bloated and moaning." George W. got down on his knees, laid his hands on each oxen's head, blessed them, and "asked [his] Heavenly Father to give life and health" back to them. The next morning, they "were standing on their feet but" could only move "the wagon twice it's length" before stopping to rest again.[29]

Under the scorching sun and with exhausted oxen, the Brimhalls found themselves in precarious circumstances. Their water barrels were empty. Twelve-year-old George H. asked his father if he could "go and get some water." George W. estimated that water was still another nine or ten miles ahead. George H. asked again awhile later. Seeing no other relief in sight, the father said, "Well, George, you can go, but you must not run, but get under the shade of the rocks as much as you can."[30]

George W. moved the oxen forward so they could stay in the shade of the rocks as much as possible, keeping his eyes on his young son, who against instructions, "was on the run" at a quick pace. George W. wrote,

> I knew that no muscle, flesh or blood could stand it long in that atmosphere, at a speed of six or eight miles an hour, much less a child. What could I do? He was beyond my reach or call. Without saying a word I secretly called upon the Lord to give my boy strength of body and wisdom to endure any strain, that would be for his good and the good of those he loved. Quick as thought, I felt he had interpreted the thoughts of my heart.[31]

When George H. reached the water, he immediately bent over, cupped his hands, and drank as much as he could. Then he filled a pot and quickly headed back. About sundown, the family finally reached the Virgin River, where they camped for the night.[32]

Two days later, George W. left his family and traveled south until he found the camp on the Muddy River. With fellow explorer and friend Elijah Elmore, George W. explored the Muddy River area. During his exploration, George W. became more and more discouraged, unable to understand the Church leaders' purpose for sending anyone to this region. He surmised he had not seen any inhabitable land since he left the Santa Clara River by St. George.

Later he wrote about the spiritual wrestle he had with himself over the predicament his family was in.

The consideration that I had my family with me and my own life to preserve were solid realities not to be dismissed. Had the committee of safety been mistaken, or had I also been misinformed? Was I to be the scapegoat to bear off the sins of the disobedient, which I knew were many and that I also had some to repent of and get forgiveness for. All were to be accounted for in the near future, as it appeared to me. That night I went to my Heavenly Father and told him my condition. He did not seem to be very near just then, but I continued to call upon him, and he came within talking distance from me. Surely I could not blame him for it. It was a horrible place. However, I told him that I did not choose to come here, and if he had anything for me to do for myself and those who were with me for our good or the good of anybody else, since I was weak and was as timid as a child, having no courage, I desired that he would take the further charge of all my ways, and give me wisdom to do his will in all things, and the spirit of truth that I might know the future, as well as I knew the past, and if I was to be lost here, all well; but I asked him to take care of those who were with me, and to see that they were returned safely to their friends, as they had innocently followed me. . . . I came away feeling somewhat better.[33]

By mid-June 1865, George W. felt his mission was completed. He was ready to go home to report his findings to those who had sent him, but the Virgin River had run dry because settlers in St. George had built a dam across it. George W. waited, believing he could not start until after a rainstorm provided some much-needed drinking water for the return trip. On the first three days of July, George W. "crept away into a lone place" to pray for rain. On the Fourth of July, it came in a two-hour downpour, and the Brimhall family headed north.[34]

The Brimhalls lost all their physical possessions during their experiences in the Muddy Mission. After months of traveling, they arrived in Spanish Fork hungry and destitute. George W. recorded, "We were a sorry sight as we drove down the street. Our clothes were rags, our money gone and wagon falling apart. We had but four pounds of flour." Not having the will to continue another fifty miles to Salt Lake City, Rachel said, "This is enough. We will stay here." There, in Spanish Fork, the Brimhalls procured a city lot "no one else wanted." "The poorest in the survey," George W. later wrote. The family moved into a small adobe hut on the property and gleaned the local fields for food.[35]

For the rest of his life, George H. acknowledged the influence this Muddy Mission experience of his youth had on him. In 1907 he wrote in his diary, "I bear my testimony to all men, and especially to the posterity of my parents, that we are more as a family than we would have been had father and mother never been called to the Muddy Mission and filled it to the satisfaction of the leaders of the church."[36]

While traveling by train across the same land where the Muddy Mission had been located, George H. wrote about his parents' pioneering efforts:

> They and we have been blessed thru obedience and the blessings will extend down to our posterity forever. On the crown of victory worn by father and mother is written "These are they who came up thru much tribulation."

He continued, "Where they walked in comparative poverty, I ride in the lap of luxury. They planted, I enjoy the fruit. The Lord will always turn honest failures into glorious success for them who do because His authority says do."[37]

The Molding of a Leader

The George W. Brimhall family eventually grew to ten children: George Henry, Rachel Emma, Omer Mayer, Orilla, Emer Mayer, Ether, Tryphene, Grace, Ruth, and Prudence.[38] Rachel instilled in her young son George H. a great desire to gain an education. His mother was his first teacher, and he developed a strong bond with her. He remembered, "My mother taught me to read in the First Reader, the Second Reader and the Third Reader and then she put into my hands the Book of Mormon."[39]

Farm work alone was insufficient for George H. He sought an education and by age seventeen, in 1869, discovered his real passion was to "move men's minds."[40] The next year the Dusenberry School in nearby Provo became a branch of the Salt Lake City–based University of Deseret, later called the Timpanogos Branch of the University of

The George W. and Rachel Brimhall family, ca. 1894. Courtesy Groberg family.

George H. Brimhall, age nineteen. Courtesy Groberg family.

Deseret.[41] George H. attended school there in 1872.[42] During his first year, he worked as a janitor to pay for his housing and tuition.[43] He also walked the nine miles from Provo to Spanish Fork to do chores on weekends.[44]

At age nineteen, George H. and some other young men from Spanish Fork cut down timber, hauled it to Spanish Fork, and built a school they named the Young Men's Academy. First a student and soon a teacher, George H. taught at the academy in the winter and farmed in the summer. Young women also attended the academy, and while teaching there, George H. met his future wife, Alsina Elizabeth Wilkins.[45]

Alsina Elizabeth Wilkins, ca. 1876. Courtesy Groberg family.

Alsina's father, like George H.'s, was also named George Washington. George Washington Wilkins and his wife, Catherine Augusta Lovett, were born in the eastern United States. After their marriage, they joined the Church and in 1849 came west with their children, eventually settling in Spanish Fork. Alsina was the fourth of eight children. She was said to be a petite, pretty, blue-eyed, dark-haired young woman—a nice compliment to George H.[46] To help support the family during her father's 1871 mission to England, she and her two sisters became domestic helpers at the Lion House, Brigham Young's home in Salt Lake City.[47]

George H. was interested in Alsina Wilkins's "mischievous antics." She, in turn, was intrigued with George H.'s "quiet mannerisms and keen intellect." On one occasion, he presented her with a treasured, "small, white leather-bound Bible, held with a brass clasp. On the flyleaf," he penned:

> To Miss Alsina Wilkins,
> Please accept this little token, nor is it free from
> faults,
> But like the one who gave it thee, it seeks that
> which exalts.[48]

Notes

Epigraph quoted from George H. Brimhall, *Diary of George H. Brimhall,* 2 vols. (n.p.: Alsina Elizabeth Brimhall Holbrook Family, [1990]),1:479, July 7, 1907.

1. His reminiscence is more specific: "I was born in the Chestnut Woods, on Canada Creek, N.Y." George W. Brimhall, *The Workers of Utah* (Provo, Utah: Enquirer, 1889), 10.

2. Brimhall, *Workers of Utah,* 9–10.

3. Raymond Brimhall Holbrook and Esther Hamilton Holbrook, *The Tall Pine Tree: The Life and Work of George H. Brimhall* (n.p.: By the authors, 1988), 4–5. The three children were Mary Eliza Brimhall (1850–1906), Sylvanus Brimhall (b. 1847), and Rufus Alvenus Brimhall (1846–1932). Family Group Sheet, in author's possession.

Although George Washington Brimhall never saw his first wife and children again, his son George H. did locate and visit his half-brother Rufus in Illinois several times between June 1907 and February 1916. After one visit he wrote in his diary, "Congenial conversation all day and far into the night. Endeavored to infuse optimism into my brother and his family. They need the gospel and don't want it." Brimhall, *Diary,* 2:740, February 27, 1916.

4. Brimhall, *Workers of Utah*, 17. Morris A. Shirts and Kathryn H. Shirts, *A Trial Furnace: Southern Utah's Iron Mission* (Provo, Utah: Brigham Young University Press, 2001), 426. The deed records of Brimhall's landholdings in Parowan are listed on pages 102 and 448.

5. Holbrook and Holbrook, *Tall Pine Tree*, 6.

6. Brimhall, *Workers of Utah*, 24.

7. Roster of Heber C. Kimball Company 1848, in *Heart Throbs of the West*, comp., Kate B. Carter, 12 vols. (Salt Lake City: Daughters of Utah Pioneers, 1939–51), 9:469–521.

8. Holbrook and Holbrook, *Tall Pine Tree*, 7; Brimhall, *Workers of Utah*, 24.

9. Brimhall, *Workers of Utah*, 26.

10. Edward W. Tullidge, *History of Salt Lake City* (Salt Lake City: Star, 1886), 93–94; "Snow, Zerubbabel," in Andrew Jenson, *Latter-day Saint Biographical Encyclopedia: A Compilation of Biographical Sketches of Prominent Men and Women in The Church of Jesus Christ of Latter-day Saints,* 4 vols. (Salt Lake City: Andrew Jenson History, 1901–36), 4:691.

11. Brimhall, *Workers of Utah*, 26. George W. recorded the year of his son's birth one year off in this reminiscence.

12. Brimhall, *Workers of Utah*, 26.

13. George H. Brimhall, in Jennie H. Groberg and Delbert V. Groberg, comps., *Biography Collection: George H. Brimhall* (Utah: Alsina Elizabeth Brimhall Holbrook Family, 1988), 5.

14. Brimhall, *Workers of Utah*, 34–35; Holbrook and Holbrook, *Tall Pine Tree*, 8; Family Group Sheet, in author's possession.

15. Brimhall, *Workers of Utah*, 36.

16. Brimhall, *Workers of Utah*, 36; Leonard J. Arrington, "The Mormon Cotton Mission in Southern Utah," *Pacific Historical Review* 25, no. 3 (August 1956): 221–238; and "The Cotton Mission," *Utah Historical Quarterly* 29, no. 3 (July 1961): 201–21.

17. Brimhall, *Workers of Utah*, 36.

18. Brimhall, *Workers of Utah*, 36.

19. Brimhall, *Workers of Utah*, 41.

20. Brimhall, *Workers of Utah*, 41.

21. Brimhall, *Workers of Utah*, 44–45.

22. Brimhall, *Workers of Utah*, 41.

23. Audrey M. Godfrey, "Colonizing the Muddy River Valley: A New Perspective," *Journal of Mormon History* 22, no. 2 (Fall 1996): 124. See also Melvin T. Smith, "Mormon Exploration in the Lower Colorado River Area," in *The Mormon Role in the Settlement of the West,* ed. Richard H. Jackson (Provo, Utah: Brigham Young University Press, 1978), 29–49; and "Muddy Mission Settled a 'Forbidding, Lonely' Area," *Church News,* published by *Deseret News,* January 12, 1991, 11.

24. In his book, George W. gives March 23, 1864, as the departure date for the second mission, but he also claims he served the first mission (the Cotton Mission) in April 1864. See Brimhall, *Workers of Utah,* 42. Another source claims the Brimhall family arrived at the Muddy Mission in 1865. See "Mormon Exploration in the Lower Colorado River Area," 41. Audrey Godfrey also says members were called to the Muddy Mission in 1865. See Godfrey, "Muddy Mission Settled a 'Forbidding, Lonely' Area." The correct year is almost certainly 1865.

25. The first six children were: George Henry (1852–1932), Rachel Emma [Robertson] (1854–1926), Emer Mayer (1856–1907), Orilla Mayer [Boyack] (1858–1915), Omer Mayer (1860–1916), Ruth Rose [Williams] (1863–1894). Ruth Rose would have been two months old on that date.

26. Brimhall, *Workers of Utah,* 43.

27. Thomas Smith arrived with the first settlers in 1865, and the community of St. Thomas contained about forty-five families in the 1860s. James G. Bleak, "Annals of the Southern Utah Mission," typescript, 1928, 180, 197–98, L. Tom Perry Special Collections, Harold B. Lee Library, Brigham Young University, Provo, Utah; see also "Muddy Mission Settled," 11.

28. Brimhall, *Workers of Utah,* 44.

29. Holbrook and Holbrook, *Tall Pine Tree,* 11.

30. Brimhall, *Workers of Utah,* 47.

31. Brimhall, *Workers of Utah,* 47–48.

32. Brimhall, *Workers of Utah,* 48.

33. Brimhall, *Workers of Utah,* 45.

34. Brimhall, *Workers of Utah,* 52, 54.

35. Holbrook and Holbrook, *Tall Pine Tree,* 19. Six years later, the Brimhalls were able to replace their small "adobe hut with a new, four-room cabin." Holbrook and Holbrook, *Tall Pine Tree,* 21.

36. Brimhall, *Diary,* 1:479, July 7, 1907.

37. Brimhall, *Diary,* 1:479–80, July 7, 1907; underlining in original.

38. Holbrook and Holbrook, *Tall Pine Tree,* 25–26.

39. George H. Brimhall, in Groberg and Groberg, comps., *Biography Collection,* 5.

40. John Henry Evans, "Some Men Who Have Done Things: V.—George H. Brimhall," *Improvement Era* 13 (March 1910): 404.

41. Ernest L. Wilkinson, ed., *Brigham Young University: The First One Hundred Years,* 4 vols. (Provo, Utah: Brigham Young University Press, 1975), 1:52. In 1875, Brigham Young renamed the school Brigham Young Academy.

42. J. Cecil Alter, *Utah: The Storied Domain,* 3 vols. (Chicago: American Historical Society, 1932), 3:18.

43. Holbrook and Holbrook, *Tall Pine Tree,* 56.

44. Holbrook and Holbrook, *Tall Pine Tree,* 56, 67–68. George H. Brimhall, in T. Earl Pardoe, *Sons of Brigham* (Provo, Utah: Alumni Association, 1969), 16.

45. Alter, *Utah: Storied Domain,* 3:18.

46. Holbrook and Holbrook, *Tall Pine Tree,* 89. George H. grew to be "five feet eleven inches tall. His average weight was one hundred fifty pounds." His granddaughter-in-law recorded, "If one were to have met him but once, he would always remember his heavy, black hair, dark piercing eyes and the complete attention given one. Yet in those piercing eyes shown depths of vision, concern and love." Holbrook and Holbrook, *Tall Pine Tree,* 89.

47. Holbrook and Holbrook, *Tall Pine Tree,* 37–38; Alsina Holbrook and Jennie Brimhall Knight, "Life Sketch of Alsina E. Wilkins Brimhall," in Groberg and Groberg, *Biography Collection,* 280.

48. Holbrook and Holbrook, *Tall Pine Tree,* 39.

"I love you, Utah Valley,
You are near and dear to me;
I love your eastern Kolob,
And your western Galilee;
I love your Timpanogos
Reaching up to kiss the sky,
And your rugged Provo mountain
With its bosom 'neath the 'Y'."

> *George H. Brimhall, 1929*

2

Early Adulthood

George H. and Alsina's relationship changed from teacher and student to romantic couple. George continued to teach school at the Young Men's Academy and to farm on a small scale. After he and Alsina were engaged, he worked long hours and late nights to build a home out of adobe bricks on the foothills east of Spanish Fork. George and Alsina called the dwelling "the bench home" because of its location on the bench that overlooked Utah Valley.[1] They were married on December 28, 1874, by Elder Daniel H. Wells in the Endowment House on Temple Square.[2] Of her parents' wedding trip, George and Alsina's daughter Sina wrote, "The house on the highway still stands where they took lodging going and coming from Spanish Fork.... Father bought the smallest flatirons he could buy, as he didn't want his wife to lift heavy irons from coal stove to table where ironing was done."[3] The couple returned to Spanish Fork from their wedding in Salt Lake with a wagonload of furniture they had purchased for their bench home.[4]

George and Alsina Brimhall with their first child,
Jennie, ca. 1876. Courtesy Groberg family.

George and Alsina's first child was a daughter, Lucy Jane,
who was known throughout her life as "Jennie." A year later,
another daughter, Alsina Elisabeth, was born and named
after her mother. To distinguish between mother and daughter, the second daughter was called "Sina." Four other children eventually joined the family: George Washington, Mark
Henry, Wells Lovett, and Milton Albert.[5]

George's later writings about marriage reveal his high
regard for the institution, which he referred to as a "kingdom." When his oldest daughter, Jennie, married Will Knight,

George wrote in his journal, "Thus another kingdom is organized."[6] And on the occasion of a friend's marriage in 1924, George wrote, "Wherever there are two honest souls with a single thought and 'two hearts that beat as one' there is the beginning of a little kingdom of heaven growing parallel with the great Kingdom of Heaven."[7] He wrote the following ideas on marriage:

> The confidence of a wife will cause a husband to out do any single [unmarried] man of equal ability. And the confidence of a husband will do likewise with a wife.
>
> Ideal marriage contemplates a companionship, not a compromise of principle but a compromise of personal interests, wishes and desire. There can scarcely be righteous dominion among mortals when one person insists on having the right-of-way in everything. Our theology proclaims loudly against unrighteous dominion.
>
> The marriage ideal calls for continual courtship.[8]

These writings may also reveal something about the dynamics of his own marriage.

Karl G. Maeser as Mentor

In April 1876, the German immigrant Karl G. Maeser was appointed by the Brigham Young Academy (BYA) Board of Trustees to be the director of the BYA in Provo. Maeser began his first term with only twenty-nine students.[9] Before the term ended, though, enrollment had grown to sixty-seven, which included twenty-three-year-old George H. Brimhall. Brimhall began to prepare for his vocation as a teacher, and Maeser became his role model. In a later diary entry, along with listing his greatest thrill (giving half a crop to his brother Emer), his greatest friend (Jesse Knight), his

Karl G. Maeser and German Pedagogy

Karl G. Maeser's influence on Brigham Young University (BYU) cannot be overestimated. Much of Maeser's philosophy of education resulted from his German pedagogical training combined with his understanding of the gospel. This unique combination instilled in Maeser the idea that the end goal of learning was to educate the whole person, intellectually and spiritually, an ideal still found at BYU in the twenty-first century.

Maeser received a typical nineteenth-century German education. His earliest elementary school studies included German language and grammar, religion, arithmetic, geometry, drawing, science, history, geography, gymnastics, needlework, and singing. Maeser later attended a Dresden preparatory school where Latin, Greek, and French were added to his course of study. In addition to their formal classroom studies, Maeser and his fellow students were expected to make productive use of their spare time; each month teachers would come to the students' rooms to see what they had done on their own.

This intense education not only gave Maeser his famed discipline, it also provided a philosophical background that shaped his teaching. He studied German philosophers such as Goethe, Schiller, Winckelmann, Herder, and Humboldt. From them, Maeser developed the sense that the aim of education was to raise people from ignorance and degradation to dignity and freedom and to develop divine gifts.

When he finished at the preparatory school, Maeser decided to attend a teacher training school rather than pursue studies at a university. Although this type of training was considered inferior by German standards, the well-rounded, practical experience Maeser gained in this program better prepared him for teaching in frontier Utah than the highly specialized and theoretical university training would have. During his training, Maeser was influenced by the ideas of Johan Pestalozzi, a pedagogical reformer who believed teaching should be based in practical experience rather than theory, and this belief held a prominent place in Maeser's classroom.

The ideals of the German philosophers, the breadth and intensity of his German education, and an emphasis on practical pedagogy, combined with his belief in the doctrines of the Church of Jesus Christ, prepared Karl G. Maeser to be the man who directly and indirectly influenced generations of students and teachers at BYU.

Tobler, Douglas F. "Karl G. Maeser's German Background, 1828–1856: The Making of Zion's Teacher." *BYU Studies* 17, no. 2 (1977): 155–75.

greatest relative (his mother), his greatest ambition ("to avoid failure"), his greatest fault ("useless anxiety"), his greatest piece of clothing ("the old red coat-vest, into which I made a pocket"), and "the greatest turning point in my life" (when his mother said, "Go to school"), Brimhall listed his greatest teacher as Karl G. Maeser.[10] Maeser's influence shaped the way Brimhall later ran the university. He believed "deeply in perpetuating anything that Karl G. Maeser did."[11]

Brimhall learned not only subject matter from Maeser, but also administrative and interpersonal skills. During his own administration, Brimhall often referred to those lessons. On one occasion, Brimhall recalled an incident from his own school days in which some students had failed to keep an appointment, and he recalled that Maeser mentioned the incident in a speech to the student body. Brimhall said it was one of the "more acute tongue lashings" he had ever heard. He recalled that as Maeser talked, one of the students who had failed to keep his appointment turned "pale, then red, then spotted," and then "his forehead began to perspire." Brimhall said the guilty student looked like

Karl G. Maeser, ca. 1876. Courtesy L. Tom Perry Special Collections.

he "would like to eat Brother Maeser." But after the devotional was over, while "some of the boys were so mad at Brother Maeser they wanted to leave school," this student, Josh Greenwood, went up to Maeser and said, "I just needed that Brother Maeser. I was not vicious in what I did, but I was just a little weak, and I am glad you dressed me up." Brimhall then explained,

Anyone who could have seen that would have recognized a prophecy. Brother Maeser's remarks discovered a great character. This same character [Josh Greenwood] has been judge of the district court. He has been a school teacher, legislator. He is now holding a very high position on the Industrial Commission of this state.[12]

Brimhall was sometimes compared to Maeser by those who knew both. James E. Talmage, a BYA classmate of Brimhall's during the Maeser years, once wrote to Brimhall, "You are the man upon whose shoulders the mantle of our beloved Brother Maeser rested and you have worn it well."[13] A similar comparison was also noted in a conversation by Brigham Young University (BYU) faculty member Alice Louise Reynolds. At the funeral services of Emmeline B. Wells, the Relief Society General President, Reynolds was in charge of taking a group of young ladies to the Salt Lake Tabernacle to represent the university. On the way to the funeral, Reynolds mentioned "something about Dr. Maeser. One of the girls responded, 'Miss Reynolds, I hear you speak of Karl G. Maeser, and I hear my mother tell of him, but I can't conceive that he could have appealed to his students more than President Brimhall appeals to us.'" To this Reynolds replied, "George H. Brimhall is your Karl G. Maeser."[14]

Service in the YMMIA

The year that Brimhall enrolled in BYA, he was called to serve in the Church's newly organized Young Men's Mutual Improvement Association (YMMIA).[15] His involvement with the organization began with its inception and lasted until his passing in 1932, making fifty-six years of continual service. In the early years, each stake YMMIA was headed by a president and two counselors. Brimhall served as counselor to Utah Stake YMMIA president Benjamin Cluff Jr. and became president in 1887, shortly after Cluff went east to college.[16] Brimhall also served as one of the assistants to General YMMIA Superintendent Wilford Woodruff. In 1885, Brimhall was named to a committee of five men formed to write lessons for the Church auxiliary.[17]

The Book of Mormon became a key text in his efforts to put theology at the center of the Church curriculum. In 1888, while working on a YMMIA lesson, Brimhall wrote in his journal, "Worked on sciptural analysis of Book of Mormon and felt an unspeakable satisfaction on so doing, and I here testify that every time I read the book I have a testimony of it being true and it breathing a spirit [of] joy which I can get from reading no other book."[18]

In 1889, Milton H. Hardy and George H. Brimhall wrote the YMMIA's first manual, which included the four basic subjects of theology, history, science, and literature.[19] Throughout his life, activities with the YMMIA kept Brimhall busy with writing and speaking assignments.

The Brimhall Family

Although he was gaining a reputation as a capable educator, nevertheless, in 1876 George Brimhall found himself married, poor, and with a small child to feed.[20] He already possessed a teacher's certificate issued by the Utah County Board of Examination, but he also wanted to earn a teaching diploma. That is the reason he enrolled in BYA.[21] To meet expenses, he worked as a janitor at the academy. His second child was born that winter. After receiving his normal, or teacher education, diploma in 1877, he became a teacher with administrative responsibilities at Spanish Fork's elementary school. He taught in Spanish Fork and in 1883 became superintendent of Utah County schools.[22] George's two little girls, Jennie and Sina, were in his classes, but an incident involving black wax prompted George to personally tutor his children at home. Sina recalled,

The Young Men's Mutual Improvement Association

Beginning in 1843, LDS youth met in various societies for their spiritual and cultural growth. However, in 1875, as Church membership grew, President Brigham Young united all the young men into one organization—the YMMIA. Young felt this society would provide young men with the opportunity to develop their talents, confidence, and testimonies.

Throughout its history, the YMMIA adapted to meet the needs of its members. The early YMMIA welcomed men who were well into their twenties. However, after 1901, the organization split its members into a junior and senior class. In addition to spiritual studies, the group began to incorporate social, cultural, and athletic activities into their program. In 1913 the YMMIA formed an affiliation with the Boy Scouts of America, and its younger members began participating in scouting activities. George Brimhall became an ardent supporter of scouting and was given the Silver Beaver award in 1931.

From spiritual lessons to athletic meets, from cultural events to scouting campouts, the YMMIA sought to develop well-rounded young men who were capable of significantly contributing to their communities and their world.

Hurst, Mark E., and Charles E. Mitchener. "Young Men." in *Encyclopedia of Mormonism,* ed. Daniel H. Ludlow, 4 vols. (New York: Macmillan, 1992), 4:1613–15.

One day on our walk to school we stopped at a harness and boot shop and asked for some black wax to chew. Then at school ..., to attract attention, as I chewed the wax, I opened my mouth and showed the black 'gum' sticking on my teeth as I chewed it up and down. This proved to be amusing and when

Jennie and Sina Brimhall, ca. 1887. Courtesy Groberg family.

father discovered I was the mischief-maker I was sent to the corner of the room and then on a chair on the rostrum by father. As a result of this father decided he would give us lessons at home so we had the best possible tutor until we were old enough to go to J.A. Rees's Grammar School.[23]

During these years, three sons—George Washington (nicknamed "Wash"), Mark, and Wells—joined George's family. As the boys grew up, "much of George Henry's free time was spent with them at the little family ranch in Spanish Fork Canyon." One who observed his parenting style noted, "Brimhall rules his boys with a rod, but it is a fishing rod."[24] The Brimhall family often went to the Strawberry Lake area to fish and camp. "Catching a fish or shooting a sage chicken was only one step involved in the sports. The next step was to properly dress and care for the prize." George also taught his sons true regard for the fish and game laws and regulations, which he meticulously observed. His motto was, "Stay well within the legal limits. Waste not. Want not!"[25] George was a hands-on father. His diary entries are replete with recorded activities that involved his children. He took them on buggy rides and taught them how to fix things, hunt rabbits, and ride bicycles.[26]

Alsina's Health

In 1883 the Brimhalls experienced extreme heartache from which neither husband nor wife ever completely recovered. During that year, Alsina had her sixth and last child.[27] The child was named Milton Albert, and he lived for less than three months. After Milton's birth, Alsina became extremely ill. Her condition was diagnosed as brain fever, apparently the result of an infection contracted during childbirth.[28] Years later, their daughter Sina recorded, "Everything then known was done to restore her [Alsina] to health. How different it might have been had today's medical knowledge been available. This 'brain fever'—prolonged and so high as to destroy some brain cells, apparently was caused by womb infection."[29] Brain fever and childbed fever were not uncommon at that time.

George hoped a change of environment would improve Alsina's health, so "he purchased a home on the bench near [their] first home, did some repairs and made some additions," but his wife's condition did not improve. He fervently prayed for her recovery, but one day she told him, "George, I am either going to die or lose my mind; it is for you to decide."[30] According to their daughter Sina, "He told her he would keep her, he had no fear of the other. There was no trace of mental trouble anywhere along her family history.... And for his little flock of six to be motherless was unthinkable." Alsina, who, according to their daughter, was lying in bed, "turned her face to the wall and wept."[31] From then on, her mental health deteriorated.[32]

Brimhall built another home in Spanish Fork near the family's old one, hoping it would aid his wife's condition. But his efforts were to no avail. After months of sickness, Alsina was unable to care for herself or her family. George farmed out his five children, ages two to ten, so they could receive the care they needed. The three boys—Wash, Mark, and Wells—went to the Brimhall grandparents, George Washington and Rachel Ann; and the daughters, Jennie and Sina, also lived with these grandparents and, at times, other family members.[33] George wrote, "My sun has set; from now on I must walk by the light of the moon."[34] On November 14, 1885, two years after the fateful childbirth, a court order placed Alsina in the mental care facility in Provo.[35] In the ensuing years, George made frequent trips

George H. Brimhall *(center)* and his and Alsina's sons *(left to right):* Mark, Wells, and Wash, late 1890s. Courtesy Groberg family.

to the facility but each time returned brokenhearted. Alsina made no improvement and did not respond.

For the next forty years, the mental hospital in Provo was Alsina's home.[36] Two months before Alsina was placed in the mental hospital, George married Flora Robertson as a plural wife in the Logan Temple, September 11, 1885.[37] This was five years before the manifesto of 1890, which officially ended plural marriage in the Church. George never considered divorcing Alsina. His ideas on divorce are revealed in this excerpt from a letter he wrote in 1915:

> He should heroically and manfully keep his marriage contract until the bishop or some one above

the bishop said, "It is enough. You will be justified in separating from her." . . .

This case is one of importance to me as it involves certain religious obligations and social aspects in which I am deeply interested. I have had to deal with similar cases, and I have invariably taken the stand with the men that it is un-heroic to do otherwise than to stand to their posts until they are released by the counsel, advice, and command of the proper authority. It seems to me that this is what the Savior did, what Joseph Smith and the prophets who came after him did, and it is my belief that the Savior would still be in Paradise preaching to the spirits there if his Father had not said, "It is enough."[38]

As far as George was concerned, he was never told "It is enough" when it came to Alsina. He remained married both to her and to his second wife, Flora, for forty years. At four o'clock in the morning on January 10, 1926, the release came with a telephone call from a doctor at the state hospital informing him that Alsina was very ill. George

drove quickly to the hospital, took Alsina in his arms, carried her to his waiting automobile and drove to his home. He laid her tenderly on a bed and called her five children. They came. Shortly thereafter, with her husband, her children, and Aunt Flora at her bedside,

Alsina Elizabeth Wilkins Brimhall passed away.[39] Despite his despondency that she would ever recover, and without diminishing his love for Flora in any way, George considered Alsina to be the sweetheart of his youth. He gave his daughter Jennie the following poem he had written in tribute to Alsina sometime after May 1909:

I kissed her lily fingertips;
I kissed her marble brow,
I kissed, I kissed her ruby lips,
And I can feel it now—

The thrill that swept away my soul
Though many years have passed away,
She is my own, my love, my life,—
Will ever be my sweetheart-wife—
Jennie's Ma—[40]

Five months after Alsina's death, George handed the following lines to his daughter Sina:

All radiance now over yonder
She sits on the throne of her worth
And smiles in the midst of her splendor
With a love that reaches to earth.[41]

But Brimhall was not without love and companionship. Flora Robertson was an acquaintance of Alsina and had likewise been a student at the Young Men's Academy in Spanish Fork.[42] In fact, Alsina's daughter records that when George told his wife that he wanted her to live because he had no fear of her losing her mind, "she told him to get Flora Robertson for a wife—that she was her choice."[43] Since Flora was considered an illegal polygamous wife under federal law, George made every effort to conceal his marriage to her from federal authorities.[44] Flora gave birth to nine children of her own: Dean Robertson, Fawn and Fay Robertson (twins), Burns Robertson, Ruth Afton, Paul Robertson, Alta, Golden Henry, and Areo Robertson.[45]

Flora Robertson Brimhall survived her husband by nearly eighteen years, passing away in Salt Lake City in 1950.[46] In addition to being the primary caregiver for their

George *(right)* and Flora *(left)* Brimhall outside their home in Provo, 1912. Courtesy L. Tom Perry Special Collections.

nine children, she helped mother the surviving five children from George's first marriage, to whom she was always known as Aunt Flora.[47] A loyal partner during all his years of service at BYU, she wrote, "Many a struggling friend or relative in quest of schooling found a home with us."[48] Biographer Newell G. Bringhurst described Flora as a strong-willed, self-assertive woman "constantly on the go."[49] She came from hardy pioneer stock and was always willing to do her part to build up the Church and her community. In 1927 she personally presented a Book of Mormon to Carrie Chapman Catt, founder and president of the International Woman Suffrage Association.[50] Flora loved the arts and encouraged them at home and in her Provo community. At age seventy-three, she wrote in her life sketch that her aim

George with his and Flora's sons *(left to right):* Dean, Burns, Paul, Golden Henry, and Areo, ca. 1914. Courtesy Groberg family.

was "to spend one day each week in the Salt Lake Temple." "I reverence these edifices," she said.[51]

In 1888, George was named superintendent of Provo City schools and moved his family from Spanish Fork to Provo.[52] Everything the family owned was loaded on hayracks. On March 16, 1889, while on business in Salt Lake City, George "received a telephone message from Provo that [his] wife Flora had been arrested or supoened on a charge of cohabitation, unlawful." On March 20, he appeared before the U.S. commissioner, "waived examination, [and] was put under bonds to appear before the grand jury." On April 20, 1889, he appeared before the grand jury, fully expecting to be sent to prison.[53] The grand jury was to hear testimony from his two oldest daughters, Jennie and Sina, who were then thirteen and twelve years old, respectively. Years later, Sina

Flora Robertson Brimhall, ca. 1925. Courtesy Groberg family.

told about an incident that took place before the legal proceedings commenced: "One of [the jurors] came to us as we were just seated in the audience. He asked if we had been told what to say if we were asked questions. My sister said, 'Yes, we were told by our father to tell the truth.' We were not called [to testify]."[54] After the hearing, George recorded,

A day of deliverance. Attended teachers association. Got my trunk and bed ready for the penitentiary for conscience sake. Appeared for sentence on a charge of having been guilty of committing adultery with my wife Flora who was given to me by the Power of the Lord in the Holy Temple of the Lord. The judge suspended sentence.[55]

No explanation was given for the judge's action except that apparently before passing judgment, he asked Brimhall if he intended "'to obey the law of United States,'" to which Brimhall responded, "'Yes, as long as I am in the United States.'"[56]

In 1891, BYA Board of Trustees Chairman Abraham O. Smoot, acting at the request of Benjamin Cluff Jr., asked Brimhall to join BYA's teaching staff. Brimhall, then age thirty-eight, became head of the preparatory department at

Brigham Young Academy faculty, 1891. Brimhall top left. Courtesy L. Tom Perry Special Collections.

a salary of twenty dollars per month.[57] Brimhall saw this appointment as an opportunity to institute innovations in the training school and to pursue his own education.[58] He was, therefore, again both teacher and student. After receiving his degree of bachelor of pedagogy in May 1893, his first promotion was to become director of the academy's high school and a professor of pedagogy.[59]

A Summer Mission

During this time, Brimhall began to comment on recurring chest pains, which one doctor later diagnosed as symptoms of a damaged heart.[60] At times the pains were excruciating. He feared that they were "similar to those that killed [his] father." Brimhall described these pains as being so sharp that a knife run between his ribs would be a relief, but added, "There is no need for 'grunting' to people about it."[61] Anticipating a much-needed rest from mental and physical exertion during his upcoming summer break, Brimhall was surprised when, early in spring 1897, Elder John W. Taylor visited BYA and asked him to fulfill a short-term proselytizing mission to nearby Colorado. Notwithstanding he was forty-four years old, had ten children, was in constant pain, and had planned to be with his boys on the farm and in the canyon during the summer months, he accepted the mission call.

Brimhall was set apart July 23 as a missionary by Elder John Henry Smith. From July 26 to August 29, 1897, Brimhall conducted the usual missionary activities of the era. He passed out tracts, gave talks, and visited with Latter-day Saints and investigators, sometimes walking more than twenty miles a day.[62] Although Elder Taylor had counseled with Brimhall, like a father, "to not try to do too much" during his short mission, Brimhall saw forty-three investigators accept baptism.[63]

At the end of his mission, he wrote, "Free from anxiety and depending on the Lord not from day to day alone but even from hour to hour ... [the mission] has been one of the most profitable periods of my life physically, mentally, and spiritually."[64] However, the night before he was released from his mission, he again "suffered greatly during the night with pains in [his] chest." Elder John W. Taylor gave Brimhall an honorable release and prophesied concerning his future life.[65]

In 1898, Brimhall became a member of the General Church Board of Education, which that same year conferred on him the degree of doctor in science and didactics.[66] He was now in a position to affect not only the future of BYA, but also the future of thousands of students and the future of education in the state of Utah and beyond.

Notes

Epigraph quoted from Jennie H. Groberg and Delbert V. Groberg, *Poetry* (n.p.: Alsina Elizabeth Brimhall Holbrook, [1988]), 120–21; set to music by William F. Hewson in 1929.

1. Jennie H. Groberg and Delbert V. Groberg, *Biography Collection: George H. Brimhall* (n.p.: Alsina Elizabeth Brimhall Holbrook Family, 1988), 184.

2. Jennie H. Groberg, biographical summary, in Groberg and Groberg, *Biography Collection,* 215A.

3. Mary Jane G. Fritzen, *Personal History of Alsina Elisabeth Brimhall Holbrook, a Love Story* (Idaho Falls: L. H. Holbrook Family, 1985), 6–7.

4. Raymond Brimhall Holbrook and Esther Hamilton Holbrook, *The Tall Pine Tree: The Life and Work of George H. Brimhall* (n.p.: By the authors, 1988), 42.

5. Family group sheet, in Groberg and Groberg, *Biography Collection,* [324–25].

6. George H. Brimhall, *Diary of George H. Brimhall,* 2 vols. (n.p.: Alsina Elizabeth Brimhall Holbrook Family, [1990]), 1:192, January 18, 1899.

7. George H. Brimhall to George A. Smith, April 18, 1924, George H. Brimhall Presidential Papers, L. Tom Perry Special Collections, Harold B. Lee Library, Brigham Young University, Provo, Utah.

8. Holbrook and Holbrook, *Tall Pine Tree,* 147.

9. Ernest L. Wilkinson, ed., *Brigham Young University: The First One Hundred Years,* 4 vols. (Provo, Utah: Brigham Young University Press, 1975), 1:96–98.

10. Brimhall, *Diary,* 2:1058, 1927–28.

11. "Review of Book 'Karl G. Maeser,' by Reinhard Maeser," 1928, in George H. Brimhall, *BYU Devotional Talks,* 2 vols. (n.p.: Alsina Elizabeth Brimhall Holbrook Family, 1988), 2:159.

12. "Judge Joshua Greenwood," April 18, 1919, in Brimhall, *BYU Devotional Talks,* 2:56–57.

13. James E. Talmage to George H. Brimhall, December 29, 1926, in *Tributes to George H. Brimhall* (n.p.: Alsina Elizabeth Brimhall Holbrook Family, [1988]), 50. The entire quoted passage is underlined.

14. Alice Louise Reynolds, "Biographical Sketch of George H. Brimhall," in Groberg and Groberg, *Biography Collection,* 233.

15. Alsina E. B. Holbrook, "Home—M.I.A.—B.Y.A.," in Groberg and Groberg, *Biography Collection,* 185.

16. Groberg and Groberg, *Biography Collection,* 187.

17. Holbrook and Holbrook, *Tall Pine Tree,* 97–98. The other men were G. H. Anderson, George Lambert, B. H. Roberts, and Benjamin Cluff. Brimhall, *Diary,* 1:17, October 7, 1885.

18. Brimhall, *Diary,* 1:34, January 13, 1888.

19. Holbrook and Holbrook, *Tall Pine Tree,* 97.

20. Jennie Holbrook Groberg, "George Henry Brimhall" in Groberg and Groberg, *Biography Collection,* 215A.

21. Teacher's certificate, as reproduced in Groberg and Groberg, *Biography Collection,* [328].

22. Holbrook, "Home—M.I.A.—B.Y.A.," 189; Holbrook and Holbrook, *Tall Pine Tree,* 70–72.

23. Alsina Holbrook and Jennie Brimhall Knight, "Life Sketch of Alsina E. Wilkins Brimhall," in Groberg and Groberg, *Biography Collection,* 286–87.

24. Holbrook and Holbrook, *Tall Pine Tree,* 61–62.

25. Holbrook and Holbrook, *Tall Pine Tree,* 64.

26. See, for example, Brimhall, *Diary,* 1:172, July 8–10, 1898; 1:231, April 2, 1900; 1:247, September 22, 1900; 1:249, November 29, 1900; 1:249, December 15, 1900; and 1:250, December 25, 1900.

27. Holbrook and Holbrook, *Tall Pine Tree,* 67.

28. Holbrook and Knight, "Life Sketch of Alsina E. Wilkins Brimhall," 290.

29. Holbrook and Knight, "Life Sketch of Alsina E. Wilkins Brimhall," 291. Alsina added: "Two doctors in the family, years later, examined the hospital records and concluded this was probably the cause." See also Holbrook and Holbrook, *Tall Pine Tree,* 67. Brain fever is the name traditionally ascribed to various forms of meningitis or encephalitis that causes a fever in the head. Childbed fever, or puerperal sepsis, is a serious form of septicemia contracted by a woman during or shortly after childbirth or abortion.

30. Holbrook and Knight, "Life Sketch of Alsina E. Wilkins Brimhall," 290.

31. Holbrook and Knight, "Life Sketch of Alsina E. Wilkins Brimhall," 290.

32. In a letter to her future husband—then serving a mission in New Zealand—dated December 24, 1899, Brimhall's daughter Sina confided additional details: "It was the day before Christmas— I was just seven then I think. For many weeks my dear mamma had been very, very ill. No one had an assurance of her recovery. But many had hope, many had faith. It seemed that day by day she grew weaker. It was the day before Christmas when we little children were called to her bedside to say good-bye to our mamma. Oh! Fay, you do not know what prayers were offered up in her behalf! My dear good pa prayed such an earnest prayer and it seemed to be so full of earnest pleading that she might live. And Fay, just as she told them, it was so—'If I live I shall never be myself.' Well, she did live and is still living, living but I pray, not suffering. Surely

she does not suffer. She was too noble a woman." Sina to Elder Fay Holbrook, December 24, 1899, in possession of the authors, copies in the University Archives, Perry Special Collections.

33. Holbrook and Holbrook, *Tall Pine Tree,* 68.

34. George H. Brimhall to Martha Keeler, 1885, quoted in Jennie H. Groberg, *Arrows in the Sun: Samples Taken from Twelve Volumes of the Life Story and Works of George H. Brimhall* (Idaho Falls, ID: Joseph H. Groberg, 1988), sec. 1, p. 1, copy in possession of Joseph H. Groberg.

35. Records of the State Mental Hospital, copy in possession of Joseph H. Groberg. The order was signed by Warren N. Dusenberry, probate judge. Two medical doctors, along with Brimhall and his wife's father, George W. Wilkins, were listed as witnesses. Although George and Alsina's children sometimes spoke of her as "an angel" in the care of the mental hospital, the hospital records reveal that she was not always an easy patient to care for.

36. Holbrook and Holbrook, *Tall Pine Tree,* 69.

37. Flora Robertson Brimhall, Life Sketch, in Groberg and Groberg, *Biography Collection,* 303.

38. George H. Brimhall to Norman A. Brimhall, January 13, 1915, Brimhall Presidential Papers.

39. Holbrook and Holbrook, *Tall Pine Tree,* 105.

40. Holbrook and Knight, "Life Sketch of Alsina E. Wilkins Brimhall," 293.

41. Holbrook and Knight, "Life Sketch of Alsina E. Wilkins Brimhall," 293.

42. Brimhall, Life Sketch, 302.

43. Holbrook and Knight, "Life Sketch of Alsina E. Wilkins Brimhall," 290.

44. Brimhall, Life Sketch, 303–4.

45. Groberg and Groberg, *Biography Collection,* 215A.

46. Family group sheet, in Groberg and Groberg, *Biography Collection,* [326].

47. Apparently Alsina's children and Flora's children were raised as separate families.

48. Brimhall, Life Sketch, 304.

49. Newell G. Bringhurst, *Fawn McKay Brodie: A Biographer's Life* (Norman: University of Oklahoma Press, 1999), 14. In contrast to Flora's own words in her life sketch, Bringhurst describes her as mainly a social Mormon.

50. Brimhall, Life Sketch, 307.

51. Brimhall, Life Sketch, 308, 307.

52. Holbrook, "Home—M.I.A.—B.Y.A.," 189; Holbrook and Holbrook, *Tall Pine Tree,* 73. This may have been only the Alsina Wilkins family.

53. Brimhall, *Diary,* 1:46, March 17, 1889; 1:46, March 20, 1889; 1:48, April 20, 1889.

54. Holbrook and Knight, "Life Sketch of Alsina E. Wilkins Brimhall," 296.

55. Brimhall, *Diary,* 1:48, April 20, 1889.

56. Fritzen, *Personal History of Alsina Elisabeth Brimhall Holbrook,* 12.

57. Wilkinson, *First One Hundred Years,* 1:339–40. Wilkinson gives the year as 1890. It was more likely 1891. See Jennie H. Groberg, *Arrows in the Sun,* 62, citing an unpublished biography of George H. Brimhall, written by Lucy Jane (Jennie) Brimhall Knight, daughter of George Henry Brimhall.

58. "Joseph F. Smith," April 20, 1905, in Brimhall, *BYU Devotional Talks,* 1:76.

59. Wilkinson, *First One Hundred Years,* 1:219.

60. George H. Brimhall, "Health Problems, and Testimony of Administration to Sick," in Groberg and Groberg, *Biography Collection,* 76.

61. Brimhall, *Diary,* 1:161, August 29, 1897.

62. Mark Henry Brimhall, "George Henry Brimhall," in Groberg and Groberg, *Biography Collection,* 215.

63. Brimhall, *Diary,* 1:161, August 29, 1897; Wilkinson, *First One Hundred Years,* 1:342–43.

64. Brimhall, *Diary,* 1:161, August 29, 1897.

65. Brimhall, *Diary,* 1:159, August 27, 1897.

66. Wilkinson, *First One Hundred Years,* 1:344; and Brimhall, *Diary,* 1:185, November 18, 1898.

"'The glory of God is intelligence'; 'No man can be saved in igno-rance'; 'Man is saved no faster than he gets knowledge.'

"These ideas heralded from the pulpit, and taught at the fireside, naturally permeated the atmosphere of the school room....

"Education in Utah has had no backwoods era."

George H. Brimhall, 1913

3

Brimhall as Teacher

From the time he was hired by Brigham Young Academy in 1891, Brimhall made teaching the main charge under which he fit all his other responsibilities. "Education is more than preparing for life," he once said. "It is life."[1] Even while serving as an administrator, including acting president and then president (1904–21),[2] he continued "to carry a heavy teaching load."[3] Franklin S. Harris, who studied under Brimhall and later succeeded him as president of BYU, said, "George H. Brimhall, under a tree would make a university any day, for where he teaches students will always gather to be taught."[4] Harris said Brimhall had two great causes: his religion and education.[5]

Brimhall was an inspiring educator and a dynamic orator who unified educational and gospel principles. From youth to old age, Brimhall carried forward the two great causes identified by Harris with unrelenting vigor. In Brimhall's service at BYA and BYU, his two causes merged into one. He fought to develop a university loyal to and supported by the Church. He believed that BYU, as an arm of the Church, had greater potential than any other university in the world. As a teacher, Brimhall focused his efforts on developing the students' characters, and with his fellow faculty members at the BYU normal school, he trained teachers to do the same with their students, wherever they were employed.

Brimhall the Teacher

After Brimhall's death, colleague Bryant S. Hinckley called him a teacher with "great native ability." In fact, Hinckley said he could not "call to mind anyone who had greater" ability. Describing him as "a technician in that fine art," Hinckley said Brimhall "had the capacity, the training, the inspiration and the understanding of the pupil." Brimhall's success also derived from his personality. "You cannot explain it and you cannot resist it," Hinckley said. It is "something that leaps from soul to soul like electricity from a dynamo."[6]

Brimhall's personality could be felt across campus. Enrollment in his classes grew. Colleague Ed M. Rowe observed, "There were few vacant seats."[7] The education classes and the leadership classes Brimhall developed for teachers in the Sunday School and YMMIA were unusually large. He related to young people and conducted classes that reflected their youthful exuberance. Bryant S. Hinckley remarked, "He had in a high degree that quality [of energizing students]."[8] Former student Stanley Gunn said Brimhall "was the teacher that taught so I could not forget."[9]

Brimhall wanted to change lives. He tried to reach even the hardest cases. After teaching a prospective missionary class in 1901, he reported to Elder Seymour B. Young that of the 101 students enrolled, about 40 percent had "bad habits, such as using tobacco, blaspheming, using intoxicants, visiting saloons, idleness and lack of ambition," but that by the end of the term, each of the 101 students kept "the Word of Wisdom, [had] a desire to learn, [had] a reverence for the name of Deity, [had] respect for the Holy Priesthood, and desire[d] to do good to his fellowmen."[10]

Helping students deal with Word of Wisdom problems was a constant in Brimhall's professional career. As a rule, Brimhall did not try to change the students by talking about their negative behavior. Instead, he taught them gospel principles and let that knowledge change their behavior. He encouraged the students concerning this issue, saying, "Boys, I have not lost confidence in you. I have not lost confidence in the girls. I cannot be led to believe that any great number of the young women in this school cannot take up this battle with themselves, and be heroic."[11] Once when Elder Heber J. Grant was visiting a missionary preparation class, Brimhall asked for a show of hands of those who did not use liquor or tobacco before joining the class. Only four hands went up. During the term, Brimhall taught "the Word of Wisdom and the principles of the Gospel." He was later able to report that he had "never seen such growth in so short a time." By the end of the term, Brimhall said he did not think there were "four in the whole number" who had continued using tobacco or liquor. He then expressed hope that there would "be a large per cent of them desirous of filling a mission."[12]

Encouraging Success

As a teacher, Brimhall always had high expectations for his students. While still teaching in the public schools of Spanish Fork, he wrote, "The less pupils do the less they wish to do, the more they do and do well, the more they desire to do."[13] While serving as president of BYU he said, "Every young person is entitled to the encouragement of success."[14]

Brimhall focused on the individual and his or her contribution to the collective. Because of this, he was often at odds with administrators who thought someone else could always take the place of a failing student. He felt that each student contributed to the success of the student body as a whole. "The absence of a student effects [sic] every student in the school. It cuts down our average attendance, and we are proud of our average attendance," he said at a BYU devotional in 1916.

He also believed that it was the school's responsibility to help the students improve their personal characters. He believed that they came to school to improve and therefore he was more lenient with new students than with experienced ones. In the same address he said,

> We are moving in the opposite direction to the educational polices of the world. I have read how that in Germany when a Senior gets drunk ..., that no police officer is supposed to know, ... but if it happens to be a freshman, nail him at once. Now, we are working just opposite to that.

To show how both slackers and achievers reflected their honor (or lack of it) on their school, Brimhall commented on the achievement of student Alma Richards at this same meeting. Richards had competed in the 1912 Summer Olympics in Stockholm, Sweden, where he had brought praise to BYU by winning the gold medal in the high jump. Brimhall also commented about a student who had left school for a short time but thoughtfully wrote to inform the school he would be returning late. Brimhall said, "So this man is broad enough to know that when he is away from the school, the entire school is affected just as when one man performs some gallant act."[15] To Brimhall, individuals had the power to either weaken or elevate the collective student body.

Alma Richards

Alma Richards was the first Utahn to become an Olympic champion. A native of Parowan, Richards began participating in track events while he was a student at the Murdock Academy in Beaver. While attending BYU, he trained under coach Eugene L. Roberts. When Richards went to Chicago to try out for the 1912 Olympic team, he was lucky to even get a spot. No one would have thought the twenty-two-year-old farm boy was likely to win a medal, but Richards and his unorthodox jumping style proved them wrong.

The 1912 Olympics were held in Stockholm Sweden. Richards defeated fellow American George Horine, who had held the world record in high jump, but his winning jump was against German Hans Liesche. Both athletes cleared the 6'3" mark, but only Richards was able to exceed it. He not only claimed the gold but also set a new Olympic record in the running high jump—6'4" (1.93 meters).

Unlike many athletes, Richards's athletic career was far from over after his Olympic triumph. Competing in various events, such as the broad jump, pole vault, shot put, and discus, Richards went on to set fifty-five records. He also served as a soldier in World War I and competed in the 1919 Expeditionary Force Games held in Paris. In addition to attending BYU, Richards graduated from Cornell University and eventually studied law at the University of Southern California. Although he passed the bar, he decided to teach high school instead and did so for thirty-one years. He died in 1963 at age seventy-three.

"Alma Wilford Richards: A Track Star from Parowan Became Utah's First Olympic Champion." *Beehive History* 17 (1991): 24–25.

Reese, W. Paul. "Alma Richards: Alma Richards Was Utah's First Olympic Gold Medalist." *Utah History to Go,* http://historytogo.utah.gov/people/almarichards.html (accessed March 30, 2010).

Alma Richards in Olympic uniform at Stockholm stadium, 1912.
Courtesy L. Tom Perry Special Collections.

He believed that his success as a teacher and an administrator and the school's success as an institution depended upon every student's spiritual and intellectual growth. "All the students in the school who are doing unsatisfactory work could ride in one hack," he once reported. "And it would not need to be a very large one either."[16] Brimhall wanted each pupil to know that he was confident not only of the student body's success but of each pupil's individual success. He wrote that he had "a strong desire to have every young man in Israel make the most of himself."[17]

Empowering weak students was a hallmark of Brimhall's teaching methodology. He encouraged those students who appeared to be less astute. He said, "Now, you who are struggling hardest and are under the greatest disadvantage, remember you are the ones who are regenerating the most power."[18] He wrote this reassurance in his diary: "Dull students are often more obsorbent [sic] than can be seen at the time."[19] He believed that many

> young people work hard all their lives, but their work is not in the right direction. Their time and energy are devoted to the obtaining of something external, when one half of the real digging and toil that they do for others would, if done for themselves in developing themselves, make them doubly powerful.[20]

Developing Students' Character through His Speeches

Brimhall became a skilled orator and used assemblies to inspire students to achieve more. Colleague Bryant S. Hinckley described Brimhall as

> not of the ponderous type who maps out his discourse with mathematical care and who moves his arguments with orderly precision to a grand climax; but of the brilliant, meteoric type who often reach

great spiritual altitudes and appeal to the high emotions—the kind that touches the hearts of people and leads them to action.

There was an originality, a distinctiveness about him and about his public speaking that was unusual.[21]

In addition to teaching from the rostrum, Brimhall also disciplined from it. He often took time during devotionals to teach students the consequences—both good and bad—of their behavior, using "the sheer power of character and the eloquence of his address" to bring about needed change.[22]

Student Eugene L. Roberts had a change of heart while listening to one of Brimhall's addresses. Roberts said in those days "Provo City was scarred with the unsightly saloon and other questionable forms of amusement." One night Roberts stood on the streets of Provo waiting for some of his friends when he noticed the Provo Tabernacle was lit up and that a large congregation was entering the building. He joined the congregation with his friends and some girls they had noticed. Roberts wrote that he had no interest in the speaker, George Brimhall, since he considered such people to be "old fogies" who "didn't know anything about life." But suddenly Roberts heard Brimhall's voice thunder from the pulpit: "You can't tell the character of an individual by the way he does his daily work. Watch him when his work is over. See where he goes. Note the companions he seeks, and the things he does when he may do as he pleases. Then you can tell his true character." Brimhall continued,

Let us take the eagle, for example. This bird works as hard and as efficiently as any other animal in doing its daily work. It provides for itself and its young by the sweat of its brow, so to speak; but when its daily work is over and the eagle has time of its own

to do just as it pleases, note how it spends its recreational moments. It flies in the highest realms of
heaven, spreads its wings, and bathes in the upper
air, for it loves the pure, clean atmosphere, and the
lofty heights.

On the other hand, let us consider the hog. This
animal grunts and grubs and provides for its young
just as well as the eagle; but, when its working hours
are over and it has its recreational moments, observe
where it goes and what it does. The hog will seek out
the muddiest hole in the pasture and will roll and
soak itself in filth, for this is the thing it loves. People
are either hogs or eagles in their leisure time.

Roberts recorded that he felt ashamed to be listening to
the speech in front of his friends, but found that each of the
boys had what he called a "far-away expression." He and
his friends left the Provo Tabernacle quietly and separated
unusually early. He thought about Brimhall's sermon the
whole way home. It stayed with Roberts for years. He later
recalled,

> That night there was implanted in me the faint begin-
> nings of an ambition to lift myself out of the hog
> group and to rise to that of the eagle. I have never yet
> completely achieved this ideal; but I struggle closer
> toward it every year of my life.
>
> There was implanted that same evening also the
> faint beginnings of an ambition to help fill up the
> mud holes in the social pasture so that those people
> with hog tendencies would find it difficult to wallow
> in recreational filth. As a result of constant think-
> ing about that speech I have been stirred to devote
> my whole life and my profession towards develop-
> ing wholesome recreational activities for the young

people, so that it would be natural and easy for them to indulge in the eagle type of leisure.[23]

Brimhall also required respect from the students in his audience. He once interrupted a talk to demand the attention of two students with these words:

> I want to say to a couple of individuals down there near the back of the room, that you want to go home and tell your fathers and mothers that they have not given you good breeding.... There is something wrong with your home training or you would not gossip when in an audience of this kind and when someone is speaking from the rostrum....
>
> As I have said here before, we are not striking an attitude of making you listen, or of making you believe, but we can make you refrain from interfering with other people's listening, and other people's hearing and believing.[24]

At another speech given at a devotional exercise, when the choir had just finished singing, Brimhall surprised the audience with the pronouncement that Professor Anthon H. Lund's choir had "succeeded in about 650 points, and lost in one." Brimhall added, "It has been a long time since I have seen the choir fail to hold the attention of every person. This morning there was a person 'plugging away' during the singing. It looked to me just like a blot on a page of a well-written letter."[25]

Another incident arose when a student stole a watch from a locker. Brimhall was incensed with the dishonesty. In a speech to the student body, he said that if the offender had "even so much as a trace of conscience and character, every tick of that watch would say to him, 'thief-thief; thief-thief; thief-thief.'" The next day Brimhall "found half a dozen watches and several pens on his desk."[26] On other occasions, he rebuked the student body from the rostrum for such things as "inappropriate applause."[27] Brimhall was not squeamish about disciplining students from the pulpit.

However, this brand of devotional discipline did not include holding grudges or labeling students. In a devotional talk, he voiced, "I know of three cases in this school of people who cannot tell the truth.... Do I hate them? No, God forbid. If they will stay here long enough we will get them out of this."[28] In a 1906 devotional on the Savior's sacrifice, Brimhall said,

> There is such a thing as standing in our own sins here. I have seen it in this school. A young man came into the office; there was a mask over his life. No one knows it; no one, so far as he knows, ever saw it; no one has heard of it; but he knows it. He says—I am labeled around this school as one kind of man and I am another kind. Now what shall I do? Brother Brimhall, what is the law? I will carry the penalty but I will not carry the sin. It is dragging me down. I feel it. I will carry the penalty. I took that young man in my arms and could carry him. But what must he do? repent; make restitution; stand up like a man.[29]

Brimhall was an educator who eased students in their difficulties but demanded that they carry the weight of the consequences that came from their choices.

He also used devotionals to give students practical guidance for their lives as well as specific instructions for their schoolwork. On one occasion he broached the topic of exams: "I don't want any credits that are based on cramming. The time of cramming is during the semester. I would advise you to study but very little for examinations. Rest, sleep and take exercise of body."[30] Finally, to help strengthen students' characters, Brimhall emphasized the importance of loyalty: "You have been the guests of the Church, and you have also been the guests of the Board, who have served without pay. I hope none of you will assume to be host or hostess." He said,

> I did not create this university; you did not create it. I have not maintained it; you have not maintained it. I am an employee. And shall the employees presume to instruct the employer and tell him how his business should be run? Is it good taste on the part of the guest to indicate how the banquet shall be served?[31]

Brimhall's Pedagogy

Teachers trained at BYA and BYU influenced Utah's public schools by implementing principles of good teaching learned at the institution. Brimhall was a chief mover in that training. Early in his career, he developed a philosophy of teaching that he wanted to pass on to future generations of educators. He also was interested in training those called to teach in the Church auxiliaries. As a young teacher, he and Principal Benjamin Cluff Jr. organized teacher-training classes in Sunday School and in the YMMIA. Teachers from "all over the Church" attended the teacher-training courses. In the beginning, they were six weeks in length, but as momentum gathered, classes extended for a semester.[32]

The development of Brimhall's teaching philosophy is evident in his early diary entries. For example, in 1889 he recorded that he found it "best to give a complete diagram of a subject first than [sic] go on from the whole to its parts."[33] His entries also show that he did not believe he had a monopoly on good teaching ideas. He looked to other teachers for suggestions, discussing with them such things as "the necessity of some special efforts being made to enrich the vocabulary of our students."[34]

In Brimhall's pedagogy, there was a difference between being a pupil and being a student. He said, "The pupil will say I must get this lesson <u>for</u> my teacher, and the student will say I must do and get this work today <u>with</u> my teacher. When the pupil is in the class he studies for the teacher. The little boy or girl does this. It is his ideal. The other one says I work <u>with</u> that man."[35] Brimhall's ultimate teaching objective was to train students to learn by themselves. He was adamant about a student's ability to learn. He believed the true teacher sped up the development of that ability:

> The objectives of any teacher should be to lead people or students to know what they might not know as soon without his aid, and to do what they would not do as soon without his encouragement and aid, and to be what they would not be as soon without his inspiration and thought; to think the thoughts that they might not think as soon without him.[36]

Brimhall also believed in being flexible. When the semester's schedule required a change in examination dates, he understood that some students would not be able to finish before they would need to travel home. He told the students that those who could not finish exams could take them at another time but also said, "Govern yourselves accordingly,"[37] and cautioned them on finishing what one starts:

> If there is any one thing more than another that causes men to be buzzy men instead of business men, it is starting a thing and not finishing it. I believe it would be safe to say that a log cabin finished is better than five palaces started and left unfinished. It is better to finish a tin whistle than to

start five pianos and leave them unfinished. Do not get into the habit of not finishing.[38]

As an educator, Brimhall hoped that schooling would instill students with hope for a productive future. He believed administration and faculty shared this responsibility, and he encouraged innovations to meet it. One such innovation benefited student Ruth Roberts Lusk, who was born with a cleft palate. After undergoing surgery, she came to BYU to become a teacher. There she met with the director of the normal school, James Lehi Brown, and teacher Hermese Peterson, who gave her private, daily speech therapy sessions. Lusk felt that her experience showed "the unique vision, flexibility and freedom which was possible under the presidency of George H. Brimhall." She observed that Brown and Peterson "could not have devoted their time and talents to this pioneering endeavor without the beaming approval of President Brimhall," and she called the experience a miracle where the dumb had learned to speak.[39]

Brimhall used the Savior's example as a guide for all aspects of pedagogical practices and said, "Teaching was the vocation of the master. The teacher's work—creative. In the beginning the earth was without form and void; so is the world to the child. The teacher is to make the world for the child, by leading him to discover." Brimhall continued, "The preparation of the material was spiritual. All things created first spiritual then temporal. Man imitates God in preparing and planning."[40]

Brimhall hoped future teachers studying at BYU would also use the Savior as their role model and that the study of pedagogy would be a priority for them. Brimhall attended the National Educational Association's annual meeting in Los Angeles in 1907 and wrote in his notes, "Normal school students should be filled with the spirit of pedagogical inquiry from first to last."[41] He attended the Congress of Religious Education Association in Chicago in 1916 and wrote, "As a Normal School, the B.Y.U. needs to exist for the purpose of training teachers for the church, the schools and the world."[42] His ambition was to make BYU the place from which Latter-day Saint teachers would go forth to influence the destiny of Utah, the United States, and the kingdom of God. Of BYU graduates, Brimhall said, "We are not the geologists nor the biologists nor the sociologists of the world—more than anything else we are the teachers of the world."[43] He rejoiced, "Rare, indeed, are the cases of failure among those sent forth from our institution as teachers."[44]

In 1900, while serving as acting president of BYA, Brimhall announced that courses on parenthood would be added to the teaching curriculum, something he and President Cluff had worked on together. He was pleased with this addition because as far as he was aware, "the Latter-day Saints are the first people in the world ... to make the theory of parenthood a part of their higher education. In no other system of training, have courses in parenthood been included as part of the academic curriculum."[45] Earlier, on January 9, 1900, he wrote in his diary, "Today organized and taught the first lesson to the first college class in Parenthood ever taught on the earth."[46]

Brimhall's reputation as an educator spread throughout the university, the Church, the state of Utah, and the nation. After he "had been an active, paid-up member" of the National Education Association for twenty years, the BYU faculty awarded "the great educator" a lifetime membership to that organization.[47] Brimhall established friendships with educational leaders throughout the nation and frequently invited them to BYU. During their visits, these prominent educators often stayed at Brimhall's home on the corner of First North and Third East in Provo.[48]

The Brimhall home on the corner of First North and Third East in Provo. Courtesy Groberg family.

Brigham Young Academy campus, 1902. Courtesy L. Tom Perry Special Collections.

A Church Normal School

In spring 1900, BYA President Benjamin Cluff Jr. left on a scientific expedition to Central and South America to prove the authenticity of the Book of Mormon and to collect botanical, zoological, geological, and archeological specimens. Brimhall, then age forty-seven, was named the academy's acting president.[49]

BYA was only one of many Church academies. Due to economic conditions, Church leaders were considering closing several Church academies, including BYA. But Brimhall was determined that the institution should become the Church's lead normal, or teacher training, school.[50]

He reported to the school's board that the academy was "preeminently a theological school," where spiritual development was part of the aim and where learners were led "to a knowledge of God, a love for God and power with God." Then Brimhall added, "Next to being a theological school the Academy is famed for its normal work which it has emphasized ever since its founding."[51] Nevertheless, to save money, in 1900 the board closed the academy's training school where those studying to be teachers practiced their teaching skills in classroom setting.[52] Brimhall urged the board to reestablish the training school and warned, "The discontinuance of this training school handicaps us in the race of competition with other normal schools in furnishing finished teachers. We are strong in our faith that some way will be provided for the re-establishment of this essential feature of normal work."[53]

For the next year, Brimhall doggedly pursued the reestablishment of the training school. When it became apparent that no Church funds would be available for that purpose, he turned to local support and began planning for a new training school building to be built without Church funds. He wrote to Cluff, "I don't know that I will be able

Benjamin Cluff's South American Expedition

In December 1899, Benjamin Cluff Jr. organized an expedition to South and Central America. He hoped to find scientific proof of the Book of Mormon, heighten the scholarly reputation of BYA, and open the door for missionary work in Latin America. The main area of exploration was to be along the Magdalena River in Colombia (supposedly the Book of Mormon's River Sidon).

The group departed Provo on April 17, 1900. As the expedition traveled south, they began to survive off the land. Then they were delayed for a month in Thatcher, Arizona, while Cluff negotiated with Mexican customs officials. Elder Heber J. Grant visited the group while they waited and felt most of the young men were too inexperienced and their lives would be in jeopardy if they continued. Soon after, the First Presidency and Twelve agreed it would be best to disband the group.

In August 1900, Church President Joseph F. Smith honorably released those who chose to go home. However, Cluff and eight others chose to continue their journey, realizing the expedition was now purely scientific and not a Church mission.

Travel through Mexico became increasingly difficult. As supplies and money grew short, personal conflicts and illness abounded. When the group reached Guatemala in March 1901, two members left for home, but the rest continued on, collecting plant and animal specimens and exploring ancient ruins as they went. Their progress was slowed by illness, poverty, injuries, and problems with local law enforcement. In January 1902, they finally reached the border of Columbia but were unable to enter due to civil war. Admitting defeat, five members of the expedition sailed home. However, one young man, Chester Van Buren, remained behind to continue collecting specimens; his contribution remains the most important of Cluff's expedition.

Wilkinson, Ernest L. *Brigham Young University: The First One Hundred Years,* 1:289–329. 4 vols. Provo, Utah: Brigham Young University Press, 1975.

Benjamin Cluff Jr. and the Brigham Young Academy faculty, ca. 1900.
Cluff is first row center, Brimhall is to his right. Courtesy L. Tom Perry
Special Collections.

The South American Exploration party departing, April 17, 1900. Courtesy
L. Tom Perry Special Collections.

Jesse Knight, close friend to George H. Brimhall. Courtesy L. Tom Perry Special Collections.

to accomplish what I wish in this regard, but I shall try."[54] With financial help from Jesse Knight, the training building—with a gymnasium on the upper floor—was constructed in 1901 at a cost of $33,000. The cost was twice the amount anticipated, but the building boosted the morale of the school and placed its normal work on a solid foundation. The building's construction was a personal victory for Brimhall, who had rallied local support, secured the best-equipped normal facility in the Church, and successfully enlisted the help of his close friend, Jesse Knight.[55]

In 1906, while Brimhall was president of BYU, David O. McKay became a member of the Quorum of the Twelve Apostles. Similar to Brimhall, Elder McKay was an educator. Both wanted BYU to become the Church's official normal school. Nevertheless, even with their determined efforts, BYU's future as the Church's normal school was far from secure. It was not until February 1909 that the Church Board of Education confirmed that BYU was the Church's official teachers college.[56]

In 1910, Brimhall again argued for extended provisions for the normal school so that the university could "attract the brightest and best minds" in the community. He predicted,

> We have not only to supply the immediate and grow-
> ing demands for teachers, but we have also great
> educational problems to work out in the light of
> the Gospel, problems which can not be solved in
> educational institutions where the field of revela-
> tion is either forbidden ground, or looked upon as
> unprofitable.

He continued, "To our minds, it seems that upon the church schools rests the responsibility of bringing to the world, a

Church Normal Training School Building, 1902. As acting president of BYA in 1901, Brimhall requested that a building be constructed for the Church Normal Training School. Courtesy L. Tom Perry Special Collections.

harmony between science and religion, and to do this we must be in possession of both."[57]

In 1911 a special committee of the Church Board of Education was formed to consider abandoning the teachers college at BYU.[58] Elder McKay was emphatic that the Provo school should remain open, and he envisioned it becoming a full-scale university in the future.[59] After Elder McKay's plea, the First Presidency and the Quorum of the Twelve not only decided to keep BYU's normal school but also encouraged its expansion under Brimhall's leadership.[60] With BYU as the Church's preeminent normal school, Brimhall requested that "all other Church schools ... be feeders to the Church Teachers College." Elder McKay also wanted BYU to attract excellent LDS students from state schools, "especially those who contemplated making teaching their vocation." Brimhall reported,

> Since the establishment of the Church Teachers College here, no adequate special appropriation has been made for it's [sic] maintenance by the Church, and the burden of carrying on the college has fallen mainly on the institution itself. We are happy to report, however, that by special appropriation the Church has provided for the maintenance of the college for the coming year.[61]

As he noted at the Congress of Religious Education Association in Chicago in 1916, Brimhall believed that BYU was necessary "for the purpose of training teachers for the church, the schools, and the world."[62] In 1920, Elder McKay, who by then had become the Church commissioner of education, proposed that "all small schools in communities where L.D.S. influence predominates be eliminated" and that the Church keep only "four or five schools with the aim of giving first class training to teachers."[63] The Church's

Instruction in the training school, ca. 1914. The training school was not only for the education of children but also for the training of teachers by the university. Courtesy L. Tom Perry Special Collections.

focus changed from providing schools for Latter-day Saint students to supplying Latter-day Saint–trained teachers for public schools. McKay declared,

> Now, if by cooperation, recommendation, and instruction a sufficient number of capable young men and women of the Church can be induced to graduate from the normal colleges and the B.Y.U., and accept positions in the various public schools and high schools throughout the Church, there should be no reason why these schools should not be permeated by a truly wholesome and upbuilding atmosphere of true morality.[64]

Keeping BYU open during years of financial hardship and eventually having it become the Church's official normal school were two of Brimhall's greatest triumphs. Making BYU a university where Church members were trained to become public schoolteachers had been one of his concerns for decades. As early as 1899, he wrote in his diary that he had visited with BYA President Benjamin Cluff and with President Joseph T. Kingsbury of the University of Utah "in regard to the propriety of getting some amendments to the school law by which private normal schools would become approved normal schools."[65] In 1920, Brimhall's wishes came true.

One LDS educator who shared Brimhall's vision was John A. Widtsoe, president of the Agricultural College of Utah in Logan. The two men shared the common belief that "considering the rapidly increasing numbers of local high schools in the State," emphasis ought to be placed "more strongly than ever before [on] the preparation of teachers to fill positions." Widtsoe agreed with Brimhall that this premise meant "the Church must possess a normal school which must be second to none in the West, or for that matter in the country." Widtsoe also encouraged Church authorities to place "sufficient money and energy" to this end. Widtsoe echoed Brimhall's sentiments in these words, adding his hope for a gospel-oriented future for BYU:

> The great Church normal school which I dream of, must be prepared to turn out suitable teachers for the high schools of the State.... I am beginning to think that at the present time this is one of the strongest arguments for the establishment of a Church university. One of the prime functions of the Church university ought to be the training of teachers, just as one of the prime functions of the whole Church educational

LDS Apostle and Utah Senator Reed Smoot. Courtesy L. Tom Perry Special Collections.

system should be the training of teachers....

Let us have a great university established primarily as a continuation of the normal school. Let the vivifying element in both be the Gospel spirit.[66]

Another who shared Brimhall's vision was U.S. Senator and Church Apostle Reed Smoot. Smoot corresponded with Brimhall and met at BYU to talk about the future of the institution.[67]

Brimhall was interested in the many issues facing the teaching profession of his era. His notes at the 1907 National Education Association's convention in Los Angeles included these words: "The lower the grade the better the teacher needed. The highest salary should go with the best teacher!"[68] His notes at the 1916 Congress of Religious Education Association in Chicago declared, "Educate all the people all of the time, not just some of the people some of the time. School should open six nights as well as six days," and, "It is piracy to pay a woman less than a man gets for the same work."[69] Apparently Brimhall felt strongly about this point. Aretta Young, an art professor at BYU, said of him, "No man of my acquaintance has done as much to give dignity to the professional woman."[70] Nevertheless, Brimhall was concerned with the lack of male teachers in the schools. He stated, "The preponderance of women in our schools is a grave mistake. It is important that students have the experience of working with both male and female teachers, even in the [grade schools]. Each can make great contributions the other can't."[71]

Public school administrators sought Brimhall's advice on securing teachers. Utah educator Andrew B. Anderson asked Brimhall to send his best teacher, one who "had training with considerable native talent."[72] Sometimes Brimhall was unable to provide teachers to fill all of the requests.[73] When administrator John C. Jacobs wrote to Brimhall twice requesting a BYU graduate, Brimhall finally informed him,

> I have been diligently endeavoring to secure a teacher for you, and I have been disappointed. From day to day I have deferred answering, expecting that I should be able to secure at least the services of a student who would do you good work, and I shall not recommend any other kind.

He continued, "I have made verbal inquiry, have written, have telephoned, but as yet have been unsuccessful.... I appreciate your condition and know what it means to be without a teacher so late in the season, but I have done my best." Brimhall then suggested to Jacobs, "Pick out some young man from your community who is apt and send him here to the Normal school and prepare as a teacher for your community."[74]

Brimhall's two great causes—the gospel and education—were fused in his work as a teacher and as a trainer of teachers. He personally strived to develop his students' characters, all the while earning BYU the title of the official Church school for training teachers. Over time, BYU's normal school produced an army of teachers.

Notes

Epigraph quoted from George H. Brimhall, "Evolution of Education in Utah," *Improvement Era* 16 (July 1913): 896–97, 900.

1. "Report of the Presidency of the Brigham Young University for the Thirty-Fifth Academic Year, 1910–1911," 6, George H. Brimhall Presidential Papers, L. Tom Perry Special Collections, Harold B. Lee Library, Brigham Young University, Provo, Utah.

2. Ernest L. Wilkinson, ed., *Brigham Young University: The First One Hundred Years,* 4 vols. (Provo, Utah: Brigham Young University Press, 1975), 1:344, 381–83; J. Marinus Jensen, *History of Brigham Young University* (n.p.: n.p., 1942), 46, 48–50, 63.

3. See, for example, George H. Brimhall, *Diary of George H. Brimhall,* 2 vols. (n.p.: Alsina Elizabeth Brimhall Holbrook Family, [1990]), 2:749 May 5, 1916; 1:370, April 10, 1905; 2:516, September 17, 18, 1908.

4. Jennie H. Groberg and Delbert V. Groberg, *Biography Collection: George H. Brimhall* (Utah: Alsina Elizabeth Brimhall Holbrook Family, 1988), 215A.

5. Franklin S. Harris, funeral address, in *Tributes to George H. Brimhall* (n.p.: Alsina Elizabeth Brimhall Holbrook Family, [1988]), 388.

6. Bryant S. Hinckley, memorial address, December 7, 1932, in *Tributes,* 94.

7. Ed M. Rowe, "Some of Our Educators," *Utah Educational Review* 19, no. 8, 309, as reprinted in *Tributes,* 161.

8. Hinckley, memorial address, in *Tributes,* 94; T. Earl Pardoe, *Sons of Brigham* (Provo, Utah: Alumni Association, 1969), 20. See also Groberg and Groberg, *Biography Collection,* 252, 267; J. Cecil Alter, *The Storied Domain* (Chicago: American Historical Society, 1932), 3:18; and "Executive Committee of the Seven Stake Presidencies, November 10, 1920" in Groberg and Groberg, *Tributes,* 79.

9. Stanley Gunn, in *Tributes,* 116.

10. George H. Brimhall to Seymour B. Young, March 1901, as cited in Groberg and Groberg, *Biography Collection,* 79.

11. "Institutional Honor," May 17, 1919, in George H. Brimhall, *BYU Devotional Talks,* 2 vols. (n.p.: Alsina Elizabeth Brimhall Holbrook Family, 1988), 2:69.

12. George H. Brimhall to Rudgar Clawson, February 27, 1913, Brimhall Presidential Papers. Following the Word of Wisdom became a requirement for a temple recommend in the early 1920s; prior to this it was encouraged but not enforced.

13. Brimhall, *Diary,* 1:33, January 9, 1888.

14. George H. Brimhall, sermonette, July 13, 1911, as cited in George H. Brimhall, *Words of Wisdom* (n.p.: Alsina Elizabeth Brimhall Holbrook Family, [1988]), 10.

15. George H. Brimhall, "Special Privileges for Special Services," March 21, 1916, in Brimhall, *BYU Devotional Talks,* 1:408.

16. George H. Brimhall, "Forgetfulness Is Not Lost," May 5, 1904, in Brimhall, *BYU Devotional Talks,* 1:34.

17. George H. Brimhall to V. D. Cram Jr., October 31, 1904, Brimhall Presidential Papers.

18. Brimhall, "Forgetfulness Is Not Lost," 1:34.

19. Brimhall, *Diary,* 1:489, February 27, 1907.

20. Brimhall to Cram, October 31, 1904.

21. Hinckley, memorial address, in *Tributes,* 91, 94.

22. James L. Barker, "Speech of Professor James L. Barker—for the Birthday Anniversary of Pres. Brimhall," December 8, 1922, in *Tributes,* 282.

23. Eugene L. Roberts, "The Eagle and the Pig," *Young Woman's Journal* 32, no. 7 (July 1921): 386–87.

24. George H. Brimhall, "Discipline," May 4, 1919, in Brimhall, *BYU Devotional Talks,* 2:61.

25. George H. Brimhall, "Manhood," March 10, 1908, in Brimhall, *BYU Devotional Talks,* 1:169.

26. J. Edward Johnson, "George H. Brimhall: An Attempted Approximation of His Genius, Accomplishments, Stature," unpublished manuscript, Perry Special Collections, 15, as cited in Elizabeth Groberg Owens, "George H. Brimhall: Inspirational Leader of B.Y.U.," in Groberg and Groberg, *Biography Collection,* 164.

27. Brimhall, *Diary,* 1:429, April 5, 1907.

28. George H. Brimhall, "Scholarship an Implement to Manhood," January 12, 1909, in Brimhall, *BYU Devotional Talks,* 1:216.

29. George H. Brimhall, "Carry the Penalty but Not the Sin," March 28, 1906, in Brimhall, *BYU Devotional Talks,* 1:126.

30. George H. Brimhall, "Progressively Aggressive," May 18, 1904, in Brimhall, *BYU Devotional Talks,* 1:40.

31. George H. Brimhall, "Loyalty," March 16, 1911, in Brimhall, *BYU Devotional Talks,* 1:277. See also Brimhall, *Diary,* 2:753, June 5, 1916.

32. J. Marinus Jensen, N. I. Butt, Elsie C. Carroll, and Bertha Roberts, "History of Brigham Young University," unpublished manuscript, 40, Perry Special Collections.

33. Brimhall, *Diary,* 1:37, January 28, 1889,

34. Brimhall, *Diary,* 1:191, January 12, 1899.

35. George H. Brimhall, "The Student and the Pupil," February 29, 1904, in Brimhall, *BYU Devotional Talks,* 1:25; underlining in original.

36. George H. Brimhall, "The Law of Creation," May 19, 1929, in Brimhall, *BYU Devotional Talks,* 2:177.

37. George H. Brimhall, "Be a Finisher," May 27, 1908, in Brimhall, *BYU Devotional Talks,* 1:185.

38. Brimhall, "Be a Finisher," 1:185.

39. Ruth Roberts Lusk, "Personal Recollections of President George H. Brimhall," as excerpted in Groberg and Groberg, *Biography Collection,* 245.

40. Brimhall, *Diary,* 1:412, 1906.

41. Brimhall, *Diary,* 1:484, July 1907.

42. Brimhall, *Diary,* 2:795, 1916.

43. George H. Brimhall to Horace H. Cummings, December 16, 1912, Brimhall Presidential Papers.

44. "President's Report, of the Brigham Young Young [sic] Academy for the 24th Academic Year, 1899–1900," 7, Brimhall Presidential Papers.

45. George H. Brimhall, "Parenthood," *Improvement Era* 6 (April 1903): 421.

46. Brimhall, *Diary,* 1:224, January 9, 1900.

47. "Brimhall Is Honored on Anniversary," in *Tributes,* 186.

48. Raymond Brimhall Holbrook and Esther Hamilton Holbrook, *The Tall Pine Tree: The Life and Work of George H. Brimhall* (n.p.: By the authors, 1988), 87.

49. Wilkinson, *First One Hundred Years,* 1:291, 344.

50. John D. Monnett Jr., "The Mormon Church and Its Private School System in Utah: The Emergence of the Academies, 1880–1892" (PhD diss., University of Utah, 1984), 142–43; Richard O. Cowan, *The Latter-day Saint Century* (Salt Lake City: Bookcraft, 1999), 80–81; Wilkinson, *First One Hundred Years,* 1:553, 563–65.

51. "President's Report ... for the 24th Academic Year," 3, 7.

52. Wilkinson, *First One Hundred Years,* 1:347–48.

53. "President's Report ... for the 24th Academic Year," 7–8.

54. George H. Brimhall to Benjamin Cluff, October 30, 1900, Cluff Presidential Papers, quoted in Wilkinson, *First One Hundred Years,* 1:350.

55. Wilkinson, *First One Hundred Years,* 1:356.

56. Wilkinson, *First One Hundred Years,* 1:401; "Report of the Presidency ... for the Thirty-Fifth Academic Year," 7; Alexander, *Mormonism in Transition,* 165–67.

57. "Report of the Presidency of the Brigham Young University for the Thirty-Fourth Academic Year, 1909–1910," outline, 3–4, Brimhall Presidential Papers.

58. Thomas G. Alexander, *Mormonism in Transition: A History of the Latter-day Saints, 1890–1930* (Urbana: University of Illinois Press, 1996), 167–68.

59. Francis Gibbons, interview by Mary Jane Woodger, Brigham Young University College of Education McKay Research Project (Salt Lake City, 1996), 1, transcript in possession of author.

60. Alexander, *Mormonism in Transition,* 168; Monnett, "Mormon Church and Its Private School System," 213–14.

61. "Report of the Presidency ... for the Thirty-Fifth Academic Year," 7.

62. Brimhall, *Diary,* 2:795, 1916.

63. Church Commission of Education, Minutes, February 24, 1920, Church History Library, The Church of Jesus Christ of Latter-day Saints, Salt Lake City, cited in Monnett, "Mormon Church and Its Private School System in Utah," 214.

64. Commission of Education to Heber J. Grant and the General Board of Education, March 3, 1920, Church History Library, in Monnett, "Mormon Church and Its Private School System," 215; see also General Church Board of Education, Minutes, March 3, 1920, cited in James R. Clark, "Church and State Relationships in Education in Utah" (PhD diss., Utah State University, 1958), 385–88; Alexander, *Mormonism in Transition,* 165.

65. "Diary of George H. Brimhall: 1881–1932," typescript, 1949, February 25, 1899, 100, Perry Special Collections.

66. John A. Widtsoe to George H. Brimhall, November 17, 1908, Brimhall Presidential Papers.

67. For example, Brimhall, *Diary,* 2:1044, October 31, 1926.

68. Brimhall, *Diary,* 1:484, July 1907.

69. Brimhall, *Diary,* 2:795, 1916.

70. "Testimonial in Honor of President George H. Brimhall," *Deseret News,* May 21, 1921, as cited in *Tributes,* 314.

71. Holbrook and Holbrook, *Tall Pine Tree,* 154.

72. A. B. Anderson to George H. Brimhall, September 10, 1904, Brimhall Presidential Papers.

73. Larry School Board to George H. Brimhall, October 10, 1904, Brimhall Presidential Papers.

74. George H. Brimhall to John C. Jacobs, November 22, 1904, Brimhall Presidential Papers.

"What an awful thing it is, when you come to think of it, to allow any young person in our charge to lose heart ... when almost the only really helpful thing we are able to give is an uplift!"

George H. Brimhall, 1910

4

Influence on Students

U.S. Congressman Don B. Colton said he had never met anyone who had "more heart power ... [for] causing others to know, to grow and to feel" than George H. Brimhall.[1] Brimhall himself described his affection for students as "deeply set in the emotion of respect, high admiration, and love" and "something that is akin to reverence."[2] He consistently expressed his affection, even when students disappointed him. During a devotional he reassured his students, "I heard the other day that a student thought that I hated him. I could not do it. I may hate lawlessness; I may hate impurity; I may hate dishonesty; but I could not hate one of you."[3]

Brimhall took on the roles of academic advisor, personal counselor, and character builder as he helped students develop all aspects of their lives and, in so doing, had a powerful influence over thousands of young people. "Deep in the lives of those students who took part in the 'intellectual and spiritual banquets,' as he was wont to call them, are heart memories that can never be eradicated," wrote

Alice Louise Reynolds

Alice Louise Reynolds (1873–1938) graduated from the BYA Normal School in 1890. At the urging of President Cluff, nineteen-year-old Reynolds went east to study literature at the University of Michigan in hopes she would return to teach at BYA. She studied Old English, Chaucer, Shakespeare, and English composition, among other subjects. She also studied psychology and aesthetics under John Dewey.

Reynolds stayed in Michigan for two years before returning to BYA and receiving a Bachelor of Pedagogy degree in 1895. She continued her education, gaining a Bachelors of Arts from Brigham Young University in 1910. She later studied at the University of Chicago, Cornell, Berkeley, and Columbia, and in London and Paris.

At age twenty-one, Reynolds became a faculty member at BYA in the English department, using her training at Michigan to expand the curriculum from grammar, rhetoric, and composition to literature. She was the first woman at BYA to

Alice Louise Reynolds. Courtesy L. Tom Perry Special Collections.

teach a subject besides needlework, cooking, or music, and in 1911 she became a full professor. She was a popular teacher, and her students founded a club in her honor. The Alice Louise Reynolds Club grew to sixteen chapters.

A member and chair of the faculty library committee, Reynolds was instrumental in building the school library's book collection. She helped raise funds to purchase the private collection of Judge J. W. N. Whitecotton, comprising some twelve hundred books. At the time of Reynolds's death, BYU's library boasted a hundred thousand volumes. The Harold B. Lee Library has an auditorium that bears her name, and BYU has a lecture series, featuring women in scholarship, named in her honor.

"Alice Louise Reynolds." Harold B. Lee Library, Brigham Young University, http://www.lib.byu.edu/friends/alr.html (accessed March 30, 2009).

Lyman, Amy Brown. *A Lighter of Lamps: The Life Story of Alice Louise Reynolds*. Provo, Utah: Alice Louise Reynolds Club, 1947.

For information on Reynolds's alleged plural marriage to Brimhall, see chapter 7, note 23.

BYU professor Alice Louise Reynolds shortly after Brimhall's death.[4] Students' feelings were expressed in the 1915 *Banyan* yearbook dedication, which read in part,

> To President George H. Brimhall, whose greatness comes, partly, from the lift which he has given our B.Y.U.[5]

Academic Advisor

Brimhall expected all students to finish their schooling and spent one-on-one time with them to that end. He believed that focusing on individuals helped him realize his objectives for the school. At the beginning of the school year he typically invited students to visit him in his office. He counseled, "Don't be afraid to come and see me. I would like it if there was a stream of you coming from time to time."[6] This invitation was not mere lip service.

Brimhall's conversations with students constituted a vital part of his role as an administrator. After a student told

Brimhall he was not planning to attend graduation because he could not afford it, Brimhall told the student body, "I am glad the student spoke to me about it. I love to have these heart-to-heart talks."[7] "Nobody comes to the office of the president to be reprimanded," he said. "That is a place where students come for counsel."[8] Former *"Y" News* editor Gail Plummer wrote to Brimhall, "I wish also to express gratitude to you for so generously sharing your time with me. I am not unmindful of the fact that you are very busy and could not be so liberal with everyone no matter how much you wished to do so."[9]

In his office, Brimhall tried to ignite enthusiasm in downhearted students. As part of his answer to a written survey about personal religiosity, a student wrote Brimhall this personal note: "The thing I appreciated more than any thing else was the little private talk I had with you in your office. It has been a great help and a wonderful encouragement to me."[10]

Brimhall often helped individual students choose courses and majors. To a young woman who was vacillating between completing a normal course for teachers, taking a short business course, or studying music,[11] he advised,

> Continue your normal work. You can, of course, become quite proficient as a stenographer in one year, but the efforts put forth in that direction, while they might be instrumental in preparing you to gain a temporary livelihood, would not develop and prepare you for life as your normal course.... If you are somewhat proficient in music, and have a special aptitude in that direction, by all means make arrangements to put in some of your time on music while you are here. It will be something of a recreation to you, for it is a well known fact that to do the thing we most love rests us from doing that which

seems arduous to us. At all events, come to school and we will talk matters over very carefully, and I feel certain that we shall arrive at a conclusion that will be for your best good.[12]

To a student who asked if it were better to take fewer credits and receive As or take more credits and receive Cs or Ds, Brimhall advised that "there was no question" that it was better to take fewer credits and receive As, reasoning that it was "the habits formed that count[ed]."[13]

For Brimhall, reaching the goal of graduation was one way for students to form good habits. For that reason, he spent time with "prospective quitter[s]," as he called them.[14] One trembling young man came into Brimhall's office asking for an honorable release from school because he was in torment with himself. Brimhall tried to comfort the young man. Through Brimhall's efforts, the student stayed for the duration of his schooling. About a year later, while serving a mission, the young man wrote, "Brother Brimhall, I cannot tell you how I appreciate what you did for me the last month I was in school."[15]

Brimhall once told the student body about an experience at a stake conference in St. George:

> A man would come up and say, "You know my son up there at the Brigham Young University?" or "my daughter?" Well, of course, if I knew the individual personally I would say so, but sometimes I would have to say, "Not personally, but I do know he is getting along fine because if he were not getting along well I should know it."[16]

If a student left school without completing a program, Brimhall believed it was tragic for the individual and also indicative of an institutional weakness. His reaction to a student's failure was one of "great regrets" because the student had "acknowledge[d] something of a defeat." Brimhall saw the failure of even one student as a failure of the entire faculty.[17] For instance, a mother who had requested that her daughter drop out of school received a personal letter from Brimhall. He informed the mother that a student withdrawing from school for unnecessary reasons caused "shrinkage of self-reliance" and affected the student's standing in the community. He argued that it also caused uncongenial feelings for the school. In this same parental letter, he wrote, "It is a glorious thing for a young person to feel in the making of their history that they have not failed in any noble enterprise."[18]

At the same time, Brimhall supported students who had good reasons for leaving. One student who withdrew from BYU early was future Church president Spencer W. Kimball. Kimball wrote to Brimhall that "the cause of [his] absence from school and [his] abrupt discontinuance" was that he "received an authoritative call to arms from the authorities of the United States." He added, "I wish to express my appreciation for the kindness and consideration with which I have been treated while in [the university's] midst."[19] Brimhall wrote back to Kimball with typically heartening and, in this case, prophetic words:

> You have a flood of friends in the B.Y.U.
>
> Your sudden call was something of a disappointment to us as we had hoped to have your valued services in the student body this year.... You will be a valiant defender of the truth, physically, intellectually, morally, and spiritually. God bless you our dear friend, brother, student....
>
> With the assurance that the Lord will have you in mind wherever you go, and that whatever road

you may take in the end you will be among the tri-
umphant ones.[20]

Brimhall tried to teach students that moral character
was more important than success. In one conversation, he
learned of a student who was troubled by receiving a lower
grade than he had expected, "that he had worked hard but
had received only 70%." The young man added that a classmate had received a 90% but was bothered by "the way in
which he got it." Brimhall told the young man not to be
discouraged, claiming, "There was a case of a 70% record
with a 100% man behind it; the other may be a record of
90% but we will not say the percent of the man behind it."[21]

Brimhall provided ideals but was not unrealistic about
his students' abilities. For instance, he said of one student
that he was "not what you might call a genius, rather a
plodder."[22] Brimhall usually encouraged a failing student
to stay in school, but he sometimes acknowledged it would
be best for the student to leave. One student came into
Brimhall's office and simply told him, "I can't keep up this
way, I am going to fail." The student had become aware of
the "deficiency in his preparation" and thought he should
change the course of his life. Brimhall advised him to do so,
saying, "[The student] had better be out working ... making a success of that, than to be in this school forming the
habit of failing."[23]

Brimhall tried to help students change from within. One
young man's classwork was what Brimhall called "just a
little irregular." After visiting with him, Brimhall reported to
the student's father, "He stated to me that he did not feel as
though he had been doing himself justice.... [And he] was
somewhat dissatisfied with himself.... He felt a sort of inner
evolution and was sure that he was getting hold of himself
better than ever before." Brimhall continued, "[The student]

was very frank with me, and I think expressed himself candidly when he said [skipping school] was a fool's trick and did not propose that any parallel event should characterize his future life. I have faith in the outcome of the boy. He is more careless than anything else."[24]

University Sermonettes

Brimhall was a prolific writer and speaker. He once wrote in his diary that he had "a craze for thinking and writing."[25] In a short speech given in 1928, he explained his process for writing one specific sermonette:

> I began thinking and rummaging in my mind and I got a lot of books down on my table and I read for an hour, and then I took my pen in hand and I wrote for about thirty-five minutes, four or five pages, and counted the lines and words in each line and found I had written about six-hundred words. Then I began my work—two hours and a half! At the end of which time I had my little sermonette cut down to 235 words.[26]

Late one night a group of students witnessed one of these creative moments. As they walked past the Brimhall home, they were surprised to see a light still on. One student tiptoed to the window and saw Brimhall sitting in a chair with his head bowed, a pen in one hand and a notepad in the other. The student whispered to her friends that the president was asleep. When she glanced back, she saw Brimhall writing furiously. The students surmised, "He wasn't asleep at all. He was searching for a word." In fact, much of Brimhall's writing was done at night. According to a granddaughter-in-law, "quite frequently he was found finishing a lesson or a talk at four o'clock in the morning."[27]

The time Brimhall spent with the pen and at the pulpit garnered him regional exposure. According to author John

Henry Evans, on one occasion Brimhall presented a sermon in Colorado. The next day an editorial writer commented on his address: "Whether his ideas about God are true or not, we cannot say; but while he is speaking, you simply have to believe in the existence of a God." Evans wrote,

> And that is true. The man has a most dominant personality—in the pleasant sense, I mean,—and you cannot get away from the feeling that what he says is true. He has a marvelous gift of setting ideas clearly before you, and of showing you the right side of them. He is, moreover, a hard man to deal with when you are covering up the meaning underneath a quantity of words, whether you do it consciously or not. His keen intellect will have separated the chaff from the wheat—if there be any wheat—by the time you have ended your speech.[28]

Although he spoke at many events, Brimhall is probably best remembered for the short sermonettes he gave at BYU every Monday during his administration and many years afterward as president emeritus of the institution. Franklin S. Harris said,

> Out of all of the many hundreds of addresses I have heard him give, never at any time have I heard him repeat any address....
>
> He was always new in his point of view, and no one could say that he would ever get behind in his point of view, and in his knowledge of the advancing world.[29]

Within his devotional talks, Brimhall shared aphorisms that became popular. Junius F. Wells, YMMIA General President, declared he could hardly tell Brimhall's aphorisms from those of Confucius and thought that Brimhall "could

Devotional assembly in College Hall, ca. 1920s. Courtesy L. Tom Perry Special Collections.

have been a schoolmate of Solomon."[30] Fern Young agreed; in 1926 she heard Brimhall speak, and she wrote that his words had "brushed aside the tangled meshes of surface thought and theory and revealed the naked truth."[31] She suggested that Brimhall publish a collection of his wisdom, a suggestion he demurred from. "As to publishing them," he said,

> I am not at all enthusiastic about it. I am inclined to leave them to the care of those who heard them. Most of them were spontaneous, the occasion and the environment lending an interest that could not be expected to carry over into print. Attempts on my part to retell one of them are attended with a sort of staleness that is far from enjoyable to me.[32]

Personal Counselor

Students not only sought Brimhall for academic advisement, but they also sought him on personal concerns they had while at school. "What an awful thing it is," he once said,

President George H. Brimhall *(left)*, Elder James E. Talmage *(center)*, and Joseph B. Keeler *(right)*, ca. 1910. Courtesy L. Tom Perry Special Collections.

"when you come to think of it, to allow any young person in our charge to lose heart ... when almost the only really helpful thing we *are* able to give is an uplift!"[33] A former classmate of Brimhall's, Elder James E. Talmage, remembered Brimhall as "a source of help and inspiration" during their student days and long afterward.[34] Franklin S. Harris recalled that he "was a most unusual stimulator of young people, ... and he could understand their problems as if he were himself young."[35] If a student expressed confidence in his advice, Brimhall would respond that he esteemed such confidence as "almost sacred."[36]

As Ernest L. Wilkinson and W. Cleon Skousen observed, Brimhall enjoyed spending his time in conversation and inter-personal relations.... This ... permitted him to cultivate literally thousands of friends and supporters who rallied around him in times of genuine need.... He liked students, and there was much of the missionary in him as he promulgated the principles he believed to be an essential part of happy living.[37]

His personal interest in the lives of BYU students is seen in the following letter to a student who had lost her mother:

The loss of a mother is more than words can express, and then such a mother as you had. We know her through you. Children reflect their parents. The sympathy of the entire faculty and student body is extended to you.... We, ofcourse [sic], are powerless to aid you any further than to give you the comfort and consolation that may come from dear friends. The history of your school life is without a blot. You have endeared yourself to us all.... You are young and time will dull the edge of the sword of sorrow.... Be brave and true as you were in school. Your mother's spirit is affected by you and your conduct on the earth. Unnecessary grief and sorror [sic] is painful to the spirits of the departed ones. Cultivate cheer and happiness, shed a radiance of hope all around you in the family and you will gain an increase in sweetness and strength of character.[38]

His interest in students continued long after they left school, as illustrated in the response to a former student who wrote Brimhall about a great sorrow she was facing years after her BYU days. He responded, "Your teacher of English said of you, 'There is a mind in which literary ability lies locked up and it may take some great sorrow to open the jewel case.' I fully believed the first part of the statement and partly accepted the last part though the tinge of cruelty in it forbade my acquiescence."[39]

Sensing that Brimhall had an affinity with the Brethren, some students tried to take advantage of his relationships. For instance, one student asked this favor: "I feel that, if you have any influence with Brother Smoot, a word spoken to him in my behalf just now, it will perhaps, turn the tide of success in my favor for my whole life."[40]

Brimhall repeatedly told students he trusted them and had as much confidence in them as a father or mother would.[41] He wanted students to think of him as a friend, and he addressed them as such:

> I take the liberty of addressing you as "friend." ...
> I shall expect to take you by the hand; I shall expect
> to encourage you; I shall expect to introduce you to
> other men and women of high and noble aspirations
> that will help you bring into reality those ideals that
> you have often cherished in your soul.[42]

Brimhall sought to help every potential student get to and remain in school. His reputation for kindness was well known, and students frequently asked him for assistance.[43] One parent wrote:

> I have always understood that the [institution] would
> give free Tuition to the Orphaned or Fatherless child
> that were not able to pay. Now our children are not
> Fatherless, but their Father having lost his right
> hand and being in poor circumstances has always
> kept our children out of the BYA. Our daughter Flor-
> ence is 19 years old is working in the Factory....
> She is very anxious to go to school [and] ... has even
> cried over not being able to do so.[44]

A sibling supplicated for a younger brother:

"I think He has the stuff in him to make a man of: He is the youngest of mothers children who has been dead for several years. So he has not had a mothers care, which is so much needed at certain ages. So any kindness you can do the family, in guarding the boy untill he shall have begin [sic] a foundation to a better life will be greatly apreciated [sic]."[45]

Brimhall secured a job for student Moroni Otto Poulson carrying the university mail to and from the post office so he could pay his tuition. When Brimhall heard that Poulson could not marry Myrtle Frandsen in the temple because he was not an elder, he instructed Myrtle's mother, "You tell Moroni to go over to the Fifth Ward next Sunday and they'll ordain him an Elder."[46]

A young German girl who was a convert to the Church became very depressed at not finding a job in the United States.[47] When Brimhall was told of the situation, he quickly found employment for her at BYU and, in characteristic fashion, assured those responsible,

We share with you the desire to have Sister Perseekie remain among the people of her chosen faith. There is one feature about it, however, that is unfortunate: her contemplation of returning because of discouragement. This should not be contemplated for a moment. No one should let loose of that which they know to be good in an hour of discouragement. That is the time to hold fast. The clinging on amid the storm is indicative of a strong character, while the letting loose would be an index to the reverse. I am aware also that persons need encouragement and we should do all we can to foster the faith of our brethren and sisters of recent conversion, and especially during the storm through which we are now passing.[48]

One student's note to Brimhall read, "Inclosed find the remittance of a dollar for the dollar you lent me for library fee nine month's ago."[49] A father asked Brimhall about student railway discounts.[50] Another mother wrote, "I have a boy 16 years old I would like to send to your school if I could get a place where he could work for his board."[51] Brimhall was a cheerful benefactor in all these instances.

In a devotional, Brimhall responded to a note sent him by a student. He said, "I am always glad to get the students' point of view that we may pass our judgments from both sides of the question. The Faculty has a point of view, and the students have a point of view."[52] When a group of students solicited him for expanded tennis facilities,[53] he responded, "We express perfect endorsement of your project to extend the tennis court facilities." He then invited them to select the court's site.[54]

John Sabin, who had been a student of Brimhall's at BYA from 1893 to 1897, commented on how much he and his wife valued the personal interest Brimhall, then as president emeritus of BYU, took in their daughter who became a BYU student in 1929.[55] For many parents, Brimhall became an important liaison with their children who were away at school. The father of one young man called his son "timid and backward" and asked Brimhall for help. Even though Brimhall found the boy friendly and "chatting quite freely," he told the father, "It would be so much better i[f] every parent who sends a child here would correspond with us."[56] He assured other parents, "We are always delighted to hear from the parents or guardians of our students. It helps us; helps the school, and the general educational work of Zion."[57]

Character Builder

A. Ray Olpin, former BYU student and president of the University of Utah, described Brimhall's unique blend of discipline this way: "President Brimhall is possessed of a stern demeanor and bluntly frank in expressing his aims and convictions—but he was endowed with the most sympathetic understanding and greatest power of appreciation of any man I have ever met."[58]

Brimhall tried to provide students with perspective, draw them away from their problems, introduce them to a broader view, and lift their spirits. Accordingly, he told one struggling student,

> It is possible for a person to draw the ills of life so close to their eyes that they entirely shut out the possibility of the entrance of sunshine. You have much to live for. You were intended to perform a mission of usefulness on the earth and it rests with you to see that every prediction that has been made concerning your success is fulfilled—that is a part of your mission.... I have no hesitancy in assuring you that universally the school extends towards you the confidence and love that is due a sister [in the gospel].[59]

In 1904, Brimhall spoke about receiving a letter from one of his former pupils who was then studying at a large university in Germany. The former student had left a job as a high school principal in Utah (the job paid $150 per month, which was substantial at the time) to finish his college education at one of the biggest universities in the world. In his letter, he likened this experience to the experience he had when he first came to BYA as a twenty-one-year-old and was placed in the sixth grade. He said he "felt very strange and lonely" and "ashamed" but that Brimhall and his other teachers had talked to him and encouraged him, changing his life. This student thanked Brimhall for helping him to "not [be] ashamed to climb."[60]

When former BYU student Arthur Berkman received a telegram from the Annapolis Naval Academy, he wrote Brimhall, who had been his advocate, "Five minutes ago I received a telegram from Annapolis stating that I failed. I am very sorry, indeed it is a great blow to me and now I regret that the appointment was given me but believe me I did my best."[61] Brimhall replied:

> While we regret that you did not accomplish all that you desired, we are sure you did your best, and, therefore you did not fail. No man ever fails that does his best. It may be a failure from other people's point of view but not from his own. Your courage is very laudable, and if you feel that you have power in the direction of your ambition and can make your way into that field again next year under the appointment referred to in your letter, by all means go on; you will have all the support that we can give you.
>
> With the highest admiration of your courage and your faithfulness and with the hope that you will be true to your higher sentiments, especially to your religion, which will yet prove to you a source of success that others without such a religion as you have can never get.[62]

When a young man admitted that he frequented a "dive" (a place for drinking), Brimhall complimented him for being "frank, and above-board" about it. Brimhall denounced going to the unseemly place but said he had "full faith in [the young man's] integrity as a student in the future." Of the situation, he wrote,

> No amount of censure or harsh words on my part could make him regret the occurrence more than he does, or do him any good. I believe that time and kind counsel will give him a chance to prove that he can and will rise above any such line of conduct.
>
> I am [m]ore interested in what the boy will do than what he has done and I have full faith that he will improve every day he is kept here in school.[63]

When a student named Elsie had a "little episode," Brimhall reported,

> Aside from breaking away from our regulations concerning parties, she has been a good student and has shown a very consistent and repentant spirit, and we have reinstated her to class privileges with the understanding that her social privileges will not be restored until after the Thanksgiving recess.

He then gave these reassuring words:

> It has not been my experience to meet with more candor, frankness, and ladylike conduct in a student who has been under suspension, and were it possible to extend to her special leniency without the appearance of unjust discrimination, the suspension of her social privileges could consistently be shortened in her case.[64]

Brimhall was concerned with what today might be considered minor student infractions. For example, he gave library assistant Emma Larsen specific instructions to keep patrons quiet in the library. She wrote in a 1941 letter to a library historian, "Once Brother Brimhall gave me some

Library in the High School Building, ca. 1913. Courtesy L. Tom Perry Special Collections.

cards he had prepared with blanks for the name of the offending students and said to me 'If anyone talks in this room have them sign this card and bring the card to me and I will deal with the offender.'"[65]

Nevertheless, Brimhall believed that former infractions or transgressions should not color one's opinion of a student's future. He advised, "Repentance changes character.... You say people forgive 'but do not forget.' The trouble is they do not forgive; if they did they would remember that the prodigal returned.... He was a new man."[66] After telling a parent about how pleased he was with a daughter's faithfulness to her duties and schoolwork, Brimhall referred to an exception that involved her visiting a young man from

Colorado. He referred to this simply as an "unwise move," and said, "She manifested such a beautiful disposition and was so womanly in her expressions of determination to not accept this person's attentions any further, that I took her into my confidence again."[67]

After visiting with a student, Brimhall told his parents he found the boy "under some very mistaken ideas ... just a little stiff and over-independent." He continued,

> I saw further that all he needs is a thorough change of idea and good society, and he will come out on the right side. He is just at that age when boys think they know everything. I am thoroughly convinced that there need be no danger as to his course of life if he can be bridged over this perilous period of the next two years. It is not often that I write in detail to parents or guardians because they do not always appreciate our labors as you have done.[68]

Brimhall sought to create a paternal relationship with each student who attended his classes or attended BYU during his tenure as president. Of one student he said, "Elmira understands that I am her foster father while she is at school.... I shall continue to treat her as my own daughter, and take the same interest in her thatI [sic] would if she were my own child."[69]

In 1905, a mother received an anonymous letter slandering the reputation of her daughter Susa, a student at BYU. The mother believed the accusations, and a heartbroken Susa asked Brimhall to intercede for her. Brimhall wrote the mother, proclaiming, "I denounce the anonymous communication as a falsehood and slander, without any foundation whatever.... I make it a rule of my life to place a communication to which a person will not sign his or her name, as a dishonest affair." He suggested that a classmate of Susa's may have been jealous. Brimhall assured the mother,

> Personally, I have become strongly attached to the girl with the feelings that a parent would have for a child.... Very few have made as rapid advancement in culture, refinement and high ideality as Susa has; and if she has in any way stepped aside from the paths of propriety, it is without our knowledge, and hence the report concerning her, in our opinion is entirely unfounded.[70]

However, if students did not change after correction, Brimhall was more than willing to send them home. That was his ultimate discipline. However, his withdrawal policy mandated a visit to the president's office to ask for a release.[71] Once, Brimhall had four personal interviews with a student, trying in every way to help her get her work done. However, when she did not respond, she was sent home.[72]

Concerning the job of expelling students, Brimhall said,

> I have had a young man called into the office by my request, a young man I would die for; I would throw myself into the jaws of a lion or in the cannon's mouth....
>
> He could not see the anguish. I had to say to him, "As your father would say, 'What I have, you may have.' ... But as president of this school, I expel you ... if you do not stop what you have started." ... That is my trial. That is where I make [a] sacrifice.[73]

Brimhall often wrote letters of recommendation and sought employment for former students. Margaret Maw remembered Brimhall coming to her hometown of Deseret, Utah, in 1892, soon after he had joined the BYA faculty. After this visit, she was convinced the way could be opened for her to attend BYA. She recalled that at one social gathering at the academy, Brimhall remarked, "Now, there's Margaret—she will bring forth Washingtons and Lincolns in her family."[74]

After Maw finished her first year of teaching at an LDS academy, she found out it was closing. She went to see Brimhall for help. He recommended her for a teaching position in Spring Lake. He informed Maw that the position would be challenging ("The pupils were in the habit of throwing out their teachers") but assured Maw she would succeed.[75]

After a week of teaching, Maw came into Brimhall's office, burst into tears, and cried, "Brother Brimhall! I've expelled a boy the first week—it happens its [sic] the boy where I board too—I didn't know it at the time.... I threw him out by the coat collar." Maw recalled that after she had finished, he said, "What are you crying for? You're in! You've done just what had to be done. You'll have no more trouble over there. You've made it girl! I'm proud of you."[76]

One student was insistent that bolstering his earning power was the only goal of his education. Brimhall's skillful maneuvering, however, caused him to change:

> Your soul is too young and of too high a grade to be weighted down and handicapped at this early stage with the secondary wisdom of the world; i.e. money-making. You, of course, need that, but it should never, at any turn in your life, be made the paramount issue. Perhaps you will never know how close you are to me as a kindred spirit; suffice it to say, I am deeply, very deeply interested in you; and, therefore, my chief anxiety concerning you is that you may grow, and grow right. There is good growth; there is better growth; and there is the best growth. I would

have you in the superlative degree, making your way on the earth.[77]

Brimhall's influence was long remembered by many of his students. A man once stopped him to say,

> I must tell you of a kindness you did for me years ago when I was a boy, a youngster, restless, careless, and came to school and you "lined me up" on the cigarette habit. You handled me that day; you argued with me, and you won out. I have been called to preside over a Stake of Zion.[78]

Similarly, Brimhall once told of a man who asked him, "Do you remember what I did the first two years of my high school in the university?" The man pointed to the pool hall. He then explained that Brimhall had made it so hard for him to play pool that he went on to graduate. The young man thanked Brimhall for blocking the way to the pool hall. After telling of this incident, Brimhall continued, "Now, this school lends means of putting up fences in the right direction, and I am going to ask you to remember that we will put barbs on them, if it is necessary."[79]

Brimhall's friend A. T. Thurber said that Brimhall was "life's unsevered tie between [his] pupils and eternity and thru this and all life many of us will carry more of Dr. Brimhall than any other man, not excepting loved and honored fathers."[80] As T. N. Taylor, president of the Utah Stake, said at the time of Brimhall's death, one of the reasons Brimhall was able to "build the character of boys and girls" was that "his heart was in the work."[81]

Notes

Epigraph quoted from John Henry Evans, "Some Men Who Have Done Things: V.— George H. Brimhall," *Improvement Era* 13 (March 1910): 405; emphasis in original.

1. Don B. Colton, "A Word of Appreciation for Dr. George H. Brimhall," in *Tributes to George H. Brimhall* (n.p.: Alsina Elizabeth Brimhall Holbrook Family, [1988]), 274.

2. George H. Brimhall, "Seek, Make, Take Corrections," April 2, 1915, in George H. Brimhall, *BYU Devotional Talks,* 2 vols. (n.p.: Alsina Elizabeth Brimhall Holbrook Family, 1988), 1:367.

3. George H. Brimhall, "Encourage the Right Spirit," December 10, 1917, in Brimhall, *BYU Devotional Talks,* 2:17.

4. George H. Brimhall, *Long and Short Range Arrows,* comp. and ed. Harrison R. Merrill and Alice L. Reynolds, 2d ed. (Provo, Utah: Brigham Young University Press, 1936), 15.

5. Brigham Young University, *The Banyan* (Provo, Utah: Brigham Young University, 1915), 8.

6. "Reverence for President Smith," October 26, 1904, in Brimhall, *BYU Devotional Talks,* 1:54.

7. George H. Brimhall, "Commencement Week," May 13, 1904, in Brimhall, *BYU Devotional Talks,* 1:37.

8. George H. Brimhall, "Homesickness," November 9, 1914, in Brimhall, *BYU Devotional Talks,* 1:325.

9. Gail Plummer to George H. Brimhall, June 3, 1927, in *Tributes,* 132.

10. Leland H. Stott to George H. Brimhall, February 14, 1926, George H. Brimhall Presidential Papers, L. Tom Perry Special Collections, Harold B. Lee Library, Brigham Young University, Provo, Utah. Brimhall became an emeritus professor in 1921.

11. Clara Freestone to George H. Brimhall, August 28, 1904, Brimhall Presidential Papers.

12. George H. Brimhall to Clara Freestone, September 5, 1904, Brimhall Presidential Papers.

13. George H. Brimhall, "The Student Who Will Work Cannot Fail," May 14, 1919, in Brimhall, *BYU Devotional Talks,* 2:66–67.

14. George H. Brimhall, "Don't Be a Quitter," March 15, 1907, in Brimhall, *BYU Devotional Talks,* 1:163.

15. George H. Brimhall, "Address Given Sunday Afternoon," July 1921, in George H. Brimhall, *Longer Talks* (n.p.: Alsina Elizabeth Brimhall Holbrook Family, [1988]), 200.

16. George H. Brimhall, "Student Interest," December 9, 1914, in Brimhall, *BYU Devotional Talks,* 1:336.

17. George H. Brimhall to Luke Hickman, January 23, 1906, Brimhall Presidential Papers.

18. George H. Brimhall to Mrs. A. M. Morgan, December 12, 1905, Brimhall Presidential Papers.

19. Spencer W. Kimball to "the Presidency and Faculty of the B.Y.U.," September 26, 1917, Brimhall Presidential Papers.

20. "The Faculty of the Brigham Young University" to Spencer W. Kimball, October 2, 1917, Brimhall Presidential Papers.

21. George H. Brimhall, 1904, as cited in Jennie H. Groberg and Delbert V. Groberg, *Biography Collection: George H. Brimhall* (Utah: Alsina Elizabeth Brimhall Holbrook Family, 1988), 36.

22. George H. Brimhall to Joseph J. Anderson, March 13, 1906, Brimhall Presidential Papers.

23. George H. Brimhall, "Don't Form the Habit of Failing," September 18, 1908, in Brimhall, *BYU Devotional Talks,* 1:192.

24. George H. Brimhall to Jacob Johnson, February 8, 1907, Brimhall Presidential Papers.

25. George H. Brimhall, *Diary of George H. Brimhall,* 2 vols. (n.p.: Alsina Elizabeth Brimhall Holbrook Family, [1990]), 1:319, February 6, 1903.

26. George H. Brimhall, "Birds," December 1928, in Brimhall, *BYU Devotional Talks,* 2:167.

27. Raymond Brimhall Holbrook and Esther Hamilton Holbrook, *The Tall Pine Tree: The Life and Work of George H. Brimhall* (n.p.: By the authors, 1988), 89–90.

28. Evans, "Some Men Who Have Done Things," 405; underlining in original.

29. Franklin S. Harris, funeral address, August 1, 1932, in *Tributes,* 389.

30. Junius F. Wells, birthday remarks, in *Tributes,* 255.

31. George H. Brimhall to Fern Young, September 16, 1926, in *Tributes,* 118.

32. Fern Young to George H. Brimhall, [1926], in *Tributes,* 117–18.

33. Evans, "Some Men Who Have Done Things," 405; italics in original.

34. James E. Talmage, May 16, 1921, in *Tributes,* 49.

35. Brimhall, *Long and Short Range Arrows,* 6.

36. George H. Brimhall to A. M. Whiting, December 2, 1904, Brimhall Presidential Papers.

37. Ernest L. Wilkinson and W. Cleon Skousen, *Brigham Young University: A School of Destiny* (Provo, Utah: Brigham Young University Press, 1976), 228.

38. George H. Brimhall to Valentine Larson, December 7, 1906, Brimhall Presidential Papers.

39. George H. Brimhall to Alice Grover, December 17, 1928, in *Tributes,* 137.

40. J. Stokes Jr. to George H. Brimhall, September 15, 1905, Brimhall Presidential Papers.

41. George H. Brimhall, "School Regulations," March 1, 1911, in Brimhall, *BYU Devotional Talks,* 1:273.

42. George H. Brimhall to George Wilson, September 3, 1904, Brimhall Presidential Papers.

43. Elmer Anderson to George H. Brimhall, September 8, 1904, Brimhall Presidential Papers.

44. Rozillie Hathenbrook to George H. Brimhall, September 11, 1904, Brimhall Presidential Papers.

45. James M. Flake to George H. Brimhall, September 7, 1904, Brimhall Presidential Papers.

46. Moroni Otto Poulson, oral history interview, December 3, 1980, typescript, 4, 6–7, Perry Special Collections.

47. Charles D. Evans to George H. Brimhall, November 25, 1904, Brimhall Presidential Papers.

48. George H. Brimhall to Charles D. Evans, January 12, 1905, Brimhall Presidential Papers.

49. Eric J. Mogren to George H. Brimhall, September 22, 1904, Brimhall Presidential Papers.

50. J. W. Brown to George H. Brimhall, September 11, 1904, Brimhall Presidential Papers.

51. Miranda Allred to George H. Brimhall, August 28, 1904, Brimhall Presidential Papers.

52. George H. Brimhall, "Come to the Presidency and Make Your Thoughts Known," March 7, 1907, in Brimhall, *BYU Devotional Talks,* 1:160.

53. Marion Harris and others to "the Presidency of Brigham Young University," November 7, 1913, Brimhall Presidential Papers.

54. George H. Brimhall to Marion Harris and others, November 19, 1913, Brimhall Presidential Papers.

55. John Sabin to George H. Brimhall, October 18, 1929, in *Tributes,* 139.

56. George H. Brimhall to W. F. Lesueur, December 19, 1906, Brimhall Presidential Papers.

57. George H. Brimhall to Mr. and Mrs. Blackburn, March 2, 1906, Brimhall Presidential Papers.

58. A. Ray Olpin, in *Tributes,* 242.

59. George H. Brimhall to Sister Adair, January 12, 1905, Brimhall Presidential Papers.

60. George H. Brimhall, "Keep Climbing," February 2, 1904, in Brimhall, *BYU Devotional Talks,* 1:16.

61. Arthur Berkman to George H. Brimhall, June 30, 1911, Brimhall Presidential Papers.

62. George H. Brimhall to Arthur Berkman, July 18, 1911, Brimhall Presidential Papers.

63. Brimhall to Whiting, December 2, 1904.

64. George H. Brimhall to Mr. and Mrs. James E. Talmage, November 11, 1913, Brimhall Presidential Papers.

65. Edward L. Carter, "Revised Edition," *BYU Magazine* 54 (Winter 2000): 33.

66. George H. Brimhall to George A. Smith, April 18, 1924, Brimhall Presidential Papers.

67. Brimhall to Morgan, December 12, 1905.

68. George H. Brimhall to H. B. Morris Jr., December 28, 1905, Brimhall Presidential Papers.

69. George H. Brimhall to George Tiffany, February 15, 1906, Brimhall Presidential Papers.

70. George H. Brimhall to Mr. and Mrs. T. O. Bates, February 11, 1905, Brimhall Presidential Papers.

71. George H. Brimhall to Thaddeus H. Cluff, February 14, 1905, Brimhall Presidential Papers.

72. G. H. Boyle to George H. Brimhall, April 26, 1904, Brimhall Presidential Papers.

73. George H. Brimhall, "Called as BYU Acting President," May 9, 1904, in Brimhall, *BYU Devotional Talks,* 1:36.

74. Margaret Maw, "Some Contacts with Pres. G. H. Brimhall through Which I Found Him a True Friend," in *Tributes,* 174–77.

75. Maw, "Some Contacts," 174–77.

76. Maw, "Some Contacts," 174–77.

77. George H. Brimhall to Orson Lloyd, September 5, 1904, Brimhall Presidential Papers.

78. George H. Brimhall, "Safety in Prayer," in Brimhall, *BYU Devotional Talks,* 2:362.

79. George H. Brimhall, "What I Might Have Been," March 16, 1916, in Brimhall, *Longer Talks,* 22.

80. A. T. Thurber to George H. Brimhall, May 9, 1921, in *Tributes,* 277.

81. T. N. Taylor, funeral address, August 1, 1932, in *Tributes,* 386.

*"Oh may I grow to love to give
And for the help of others live;
May sweetest joy be mine to know
That I have lessened others' woe.*

*May life eternal be my share
Under my Redeemer's care,
With those I love—eternal joy,
Eternal work in God's employ."*

George H. Brimhall, 1910

5

Brimhall's Administration at BYU

Brimhall was very close to Warren and Wilson Dusenberry, the brothers who began what became Brigham Young Academy, and with Karl G. Maeser, who succeeded the Dusenberry brothers. But his relationship with Benjamin Cluff Jr., the president of the academy during Brimhall's entire tenure as a teacher, was even closer. Cluff was five years younger than Brimhall, but he always respected Cluff as a leader. Cluff was the man who hired Brimhall in 1891 and who twice turned the reigns of the school over to him—once when Cluff was at the University of Michigan (1893–94) and again when Cluff left for nearly two years to lead the South American expedition (1900–1902). Brimhall's loyalty to Cluff was unwavering. In Cluff's absence, Brimhall led the school with great energy and eagerness, but it exacted a toll on his health.

Health Problems

Not only before and after his short-term mission to Colorado in 1897, but throughout his career as a teacher and administrator, Brimhall was plagued by health problems. He sometimes described his health problems in his diary:

> Not feeling very well, in fact I often stagger and run against things.[1]

> Organized my classes and gave them preparation. My eyes are sore. Have a boil on or in the right one, it is terribly inflamed. I have had a bad cough. My heart seems to trouble me. I am nervous and feel somewhat depressed and discouraged about my health. Am anxious as to how little ones will feel if I am unable to work.

> Taught in B.Y.A. but I feel as if I would like so much just to go home and go to bed. The man may be ill but the teacher must always be well.[2]

How much his students and colleagues were aware of these problems is unclear, but he did sometimes speak of them, usually to encourage others. In 1924, for example, he wrote his friend Elder Orson F. Whitney—who was apparently suffering serious health problems of his own at the time—about a dream he had had earlier in life. Prior to the dream, Brimhall told Whitney, "Many a sunset brought from me the inward exclamation, 'Thank God I'm one day nearer to the end,'" but the dream gave him "comfort and courage." Brimhall explained that in the dream he found himself on the slope of Mount Timpanogos, climbing through deep snow to the top. He continued,

> The wind blew my hat off and whipped my coat to shreds. So steep and slippery became the slope that I could not stand but crawled, clinging to the ice. I wore out my gloves, my finger nails and the flesh from off my finger tips. My shoes were full of holes and my overalls and trousers were frazzled half way

to my knees. I dared not look back but di[d] look upward and forward. I reached the top of one ice-slide to find myself facing another. My heart sank and but for the memory of what I had done I should have despaired. I resolved to climb on, to do my best, and leave the rest with the Lord, and then in my dream I was caught by some power invisible, except to the feelings, and literally lifted over the top to fields of flowers, forests of pine, and running brooks, and what was most wholly unexpected, a group of my brethren engaged in some constructive work.

I awoke and resolved anew to fulfill the prediction of Apostle Owen Woodruff that I should get well and be of service when most men said, "He is done for." I said to myself, "Climb on for the Lord will lift you over when the crisis comes."

I have belief in science; I have confidence in will power; I appreciate the sustaining force of social sympathy; and I have implicit faith in the miracle-waking power of God and I am deeply impressed with the feeling that thru the manifestation of that power you will receive a renewal of physical strength that will come close to the buoyancy of youth.[3]

Twenty-two years earlier in 1902, while he was the acting president of BYA, Brimhall became very ill, likely from stress. In February 1902, Benjamin Cluff Jr. returned from the South American expedition, and Brimhall turned the reins of the school back to him. Brimhall became so ill he felt his work had ended.[4] Church President Joseph F. Smith advised him to spend some time away from work, saying he should rest and get some medical attention.[5]

Following counsel, George headed to northern California to spend time with his son Mark, who was serving a

George H. Brimhall *(right)* and his son Mark, in
California, ca. 1902. George visited southern California to spend time with his son and rest from his
illnesses. Courtesy Groberg family.

mission.[6] Moving to Ocean Park in southern California, to what he called Sunny Side Cottage, George often found himself "dream[ing] of home."[7] Part of his homesickness was relieved by the presence of his daughter Afton, age seven. He wrote in his diary one day that he sang "nursery rhymes to [her] in [the] morning."[8] Afton liked to talk to her father and would wash the dishes and sweep the home "just like a woman."[9] Other than being with Afton and his missionary son Mark, George's "days were occupied with therapy, massages, mild exercise, sunbaths, salt-glow treatment and medication. On his better days he wrote short notes to his family. But the pains in his back, chest and abdomen hung on, as did his nose-bleeding."[10] Sometimes after a meal George would have to have his stomach pumped.[11] When he could not sleep, he would sing hymns in his mind. He once said that the song "A Poor Wayfaring Man of Grief" was his opiate.[12]

During this period he also wrote scores of poems that he said "rushed on me when I was too ill to be doing anything." At the end of 1902 he put them together in a booklet for his family, writing, "It may be that some of my children will be interested in them simply because they were written by their father."[13] They undoubtedly served as part of his therapy and give evidence that this period of supposed inaction also may have served as a period of spiritual preparation for the work that lay ahead of him as illustrated by the following poem, which he titled "Invocation":

> Oh Father friend, my God above
> My soul goes out to thee in love
> That I am here, that I am free
> Is due to thee, is due to thee.
>
> That I can breathe and sleep
> And wake and feel and think

That I can light and beauty see
is due to thee, is due to thee.

I can not make a grass blade grow
Or cause a single spark to glow
The means I use, the air and sea
Are all from thee, are all from thee.

The hopes I have, the joys I know
The weight of each consec[u]tive woe
Yea, everything that's good for me
Is due to thee, is due to thee.[14]

Even in California, his first wife's hopeless situation plagued him along with his own health. On Christmas Day, 1902, he wrote the following poem:

If I could make but just one wish
And it would granted be,
If I could make a single gift
A-top my Christmas tree,
I would not ask for wealth;
And though I am in quest of it
I would not ask for health.
There suffers yet another,
Dearer than life to me:
Darling wife—a mother
I'd ask that she be free,
To share my pleasures.
Drink deep of all my joys;
And with these other treasures
Our grown-up girls and boys.[15]

For the next few months, George hoped his health would improve, but his journal entries divulge little change. He wrote, "Ill at 520 Los Angeles California. Could get discouraged but I won't." In October the prognosis by his doctors could have caused discouragement. At this time, Brimhall weighed just 137 pounds and his blood analysis found "1 white cell to 40 red. Quantity 40 percent of normal." By April 22, 1903, he wrote, "Just one year since I left home. My improvement has been mostly hope."[16] However, three days later George experienced a dream that told him his days in California were limited. His son Mark wrote of the incident,

> On the morning of the 25th of April 1903, Pa said to me: "I think we will be going home very soon ... I had a dream last night that something has happened at home ... I know it is very serious. We will hear today about it." I brushed it off, ... saying, "Oh, just a dream." Well, not many hours passed when we received a telegram from home informing us that baby Alta was killed by a wagon crushing her ... [sic] Immediately I bought two tickets for Provo, Utah.[17]

Alsina Elisabeth Brimhall as a student at Brigham Young Academy, ca. 1898. Courtesy Groberg family.

After his daughter's funeral, George visited his married daughters, Jennie and Sina, in Alberta, Canada.[18] Jennie had married Will Knight, second son of Jesse Knight,

Lucy Jane (Jennie) Brimhall Knight

George Brimhall's first child, Lucy Jane (born December 13, 1875), was affectionately called Jennie. She graduated from Brigham Young Academy in 1895, taught school in Bluff City, Utah, and returned to BYA to teach the third and fourth grades in fall 1896.

In 1898 (at age twenty-two), she and her friend and schoolmate Inez Knight made plans for a trip abroad. When Jennie's bishop, J. B. Keeler, heard about this, he proposed that they go to Europe as missionaries. Aside from married sisters who sometimes accompanied their husbands on missions, there previously had been no sister missionaries sent to proselyte for the Church. Jennie had always followed the counsel of her leaders, so without hesitation replied that she would serve if formally called. Bishop Keeler wrote to President Wilford Woodruff, and a subsequent letter from the First Presidency authorized President Edward Partridge of the Utah Stake to set apart the two women to serve in Great Britain as the first LDS single sister missionaries. They departed for England April 2, 1898. They were assigned to labor in the Cheltenham area "doing all things required of male missionaries. . . .: visiting, tracting, preaching, and exerting themselves to the utmost to spread . . . the truth." They spoke in open-air and cottage meetings, knocked on doors, and

Lucy Jane (Jennie) Brimhall Knight in her wedding gown, 1899. Courtesy Groberg family.

visited other conferences to allay anti-Mormon prejudice about polygamy.

President George Q. Cannon of the First Presidency had issued a call for "wise and prudent women" to serve in the mission field. Jennie assisted the First Presidency in carrying out this decision and counseled with the presidency of the European mission on the subject, but her fondest memories were of teaching. Her first experience speaking to a large group came the day after she arrived in Liverpool. Assigned to speak in a crowded hall of curious Britains, Jennie refused to be intimidated. According to Orson F. Whitney, her words were listened to "with rapt attention" as she delivered her message with "intelligence and sincerity."

Inez Knight, Jennie's missionary companion, wrote that "So effective was her testimony that after twenty years an unbeliever who listened to her speak wrote, saying he could never forget her sincere, guileless expression and was led further to investigate and receive the blessings of membership."

During their mission, Jennie and Inez were given permission to travel on the continent with a small party including Jesse William "Will" Knight, Inez's brother, who was also a British missionary. After Jennie was released from her mission and returned to Utah, she and Will were married in the Salt Lake Temple on January 18, 1899. The young couple were pioneers in Raymond, Alberta, Canada, and later made their home in Provo, Utah. Jennie served as first counselor to Relief Society General President Clarissa S. Williams from 1921 to 1928, wrote articles for the *Relief Society Magazine,* and served as assistant matron in the Salt Lake Temple while her husband served in that temple presidency from 1944 to 1947.

Allen, Inez Knight. "Jennie Brimhall Knight." *Relief Society Magazine* 15 (December 1928): 645–48.

Mangum, Diane L. "The First Sister Missionaries." *Ensign* 20 (July 1980): 65.

Whitney, Orson Ferguson. *History of Utah,* 4:610–15. Salt Lake City: George Q. Cannon and Sons, 1904.

shortly after serving as one of the first LDS sister mission-aries in England.[19] Sina had married Lafayette H. Holbrook. Both families had joined a new Latter-day Saint colony in Canada as newlyweds.[20] While visiting his daughters in Canada and still struggling with illness, he wrote, "Health is wealth!"[21]

In December 1903, while still in Canada, Brimhall received a letter from President Joseph F. Smith asking him to be acting president of BYU.[22] Brimhall told his col-leagues at the school, "The University needs a strong, young man at its head. I have neither strength nor youth." A few months later, he told the student body, "If it had not been for the 'temporary' part I should have refused."[23] But Brim-hall accepted the call as acting president. Apparently the board also was concerned about his health, and for that reason they had asked him to be acting president only.[24] However, on April 16, 1904, a frail, fifty-one-year-old George Henry Brimhall was inaugurated as the second president of the newly named BYU.[25] His health began to improve. He attributed it to God and went forward at a strenuous pace.[26]

Brimhall's Administration

Brimhall became president of Brigham Young University at a pivotal time and helped continue the growth of the school from a small academy into a university. During the admin-istration of President Benjamin Cluff Jr., the school had grown to include a college, a normal school for teacher train-ing, a high school, a commercial school, a school of music, and a school of arts and industries.[27] Cluff had succeeded in getting its name changed from Brigham Young Academy to Brigham Young University in 1903.[28]

Brimhall's leadership shaped the school in lasting ways. Among these was the expansion of university buildings to the upper (present) campus, the inclusion of the general

Church leadership in the decision-making processes of the school, and an increase in student population.[29] He had a vision of where he wanted to take the school but was forced to accommodate that vision with factors such as conflict between academic freedom and the goals of a Church-sponsored school and the advent of World War I. He was essentially a Church educator and saw everything from the point of view of strengthening the Church.

Relations with Faculty

The General Church Board of Education requested that two counselors be named to work with Brimhall,[30] following the Church's governance structure. The posts were filled by close friends and colleagues at the university: Joseph B. Keeler, a theology[31] teacher who in 1908 began serving as president of the Utah Stake;[32] and Edwin S. Hinckley, an education and geology teacher[33] who was released eleven years later when he left BYU to become superintendent of the State Industrial School at Ogden.[34] Hinckley's replacement, Amos N. Merrill, also a teacher at BYU,[35] served as second counselor for the last years of Brimhall's administration. Brimhall and his counselors ran the school as a presidency, acting in

Joseph B. Keeler, first counselor to President Brimhall, ca. 1910. Courtesy L. Tom Perry Special Collections.

Edwin S. Hinckley, second counselor to President Brimhall,
ca. 1910. Courtesy L. Tom Perry
Special Collections.

Amos N. Merrill, second counselor
to President Brimhall. Courtesy
L. Tom Perry Special Collections.

unity on all administrative matters. While this likely followed the pattern of previous administrations,[36] none of
Brimhall's successors had counselors.[37]

Both counselors were very supportive of Brimhall, and
he, in turn, honored them. In addition to their teaching
responsibilities, Keeler oversaw the school's finances and
Hinckley seemed ever present to help Brimhall when his
physical strength failed.[38]

The bonds of respect and friendship that existed
between Brimhall and his two counselors were typical of the
bonds Brimhall developed with others with whom he worked
closely. Former university president Ernest L. Wilkinson
said that Brimhall "was a combination of both Maeser and
Cluff. While these two men never got along with each other,

Brimhall got along with both."[39] Brimhall's esteem for Maeser was legendary,[40] and Brimhall's support and admiration for Cluff was similar. "I never feared to follow where [Cluff] led," he told the BYU student body, professing, "His character to me was gold-like."[41] Over many years of association with Church leaders, the school, and the Provo community, Brimhall built friendships that greatly helped him administer the affairs of the university.

Because he had been a faculty member, he well understood the experiences and perspectives of faculty. He listened to teachers' problems and concerns in order to help them grow both professionally and personally. Instead of pressuring them or delivering edicts to them, he counseled with them. In a graduation address, he advised, "In conversation, be content with half of the time."[42] When students criticized teachers, Brimhall supported his faculty. For instance, when a student named Lafayette complained about a teacher, a Brother Warnick, to his mother, Brimhall dismissed the accusation. He counseled the mother,

> Do not be down-hearted with regard to this, neither hold any feelings against Lafayettes [sic] teacher, Brother Warnick, because I am sure that he has nothing whatever against the boy in a personal way. He has done simply what he has thought to be his duty as a professor.[43]

In a recommendation for a job with another school, Brimhall described one of his professors, Chester Snow, as "one of the ablest educators in Physics and Mathematics within the range of [his] acquaintance." With typical loyalty to his faculty, Brimhall stated, if Snow had a fault "as a teacher" it was that his professional industry left "no time for social activities," because Snow's "laboratory and class room were his abiding places almost night and day." Brimhall added,

Harvey Fletcher

Harvey Fletcher was born in Provo, Utah, in 1884. He attended high school at Brigham Young Academy and received his bachelor of science degree from BYU in 1907. While a student he helped survey the location for the block Y on Y Mountain. He taught physics and math at BYU for one year; then, in 1908, he and his new wife, Lorena Chipman, moved to Chicago in hopes of enrolling in the University of Chicago's graduate physics program. When it was concluded that his preparation at BYU was inadequate for the graduate program, Professor Robert Millikan intervened to enroll Fletcher as a special student to study in both the undergraduate and graduate physics programs. Fletcher worked with Professor Millikan to measure the charge of an electron using the oil drop experiment for which Millikan was awarded the Nobel Prize for physics in 1923. Fletcher earned the first PhD summa cum laude granted by the University of Chicago.

In 1911, Fletcher returned to BYU, where, for a time, he was the only faculty member with a PhD. Later, he became director of research at Bell Labs in New York City, where he became known as the father of stereophonic sound and was a key contributor to the development of the audiometer and the electronic hearing aid, along with many other tools to improve speech transmission and sound recordings. He returned to BYU in 1953 as founding dean of the engineering department, renamed the Ira A. Fulton College of Engineering and Technology in 2003.

"Harvey Fletcher: Scientist, Father of Stereophonic Sound, Author." *Brigham Young High School.* http://byhigh.org/History/Fletcher/DrHarvey.html.

"History of the College." *Brigham Young University Ira A. Fulton College of Engineering and Technology.* http://www.et.byu.edu/college_history.htm.

"He can be counted on as a man of lofty ideals and as one deserving the confidence of administrative officers."[44]

Brimhall wanted the best teachers and the latest teachings. He read often and was open to new ideas, but at heart he was a down-to-earth man who relied more on what he learned from his frontier upbringing than from his book studies. This was apparent in a meeting with Professor Harvey Fletcher, who later gained renown as a physicist at Bell Laboratories. Fletcher recalled that he was asked to come to "Brimhall's office for a conference." Fletcher wrote, "Four of the older students in my class were there as a committee complaing [sic] that I was teaching false laws of physics." The students had a problem with a statement Fletcher had made in class about action and reaction. He had said, "When a pair of horses were pulling a wagon down the street, the wagon pulled back with just the same force that the horses pulled forward." The students countered, "Any simpleton could see that the wagon would not move under those circumstances." Fletcher argued with President Brimhall, the students, and a chemistry professor who also was in attendance at the meeting that this was "a very fundamental law in physics and [his] statement represented the basic fact in mechanics and dynamics ... but to no avail." The last words Fletcher heard from Brimhall

Harvey Fletcher whitewashing the Y as a student at BYU, 1906 or 1907. Courtesy Tom Fletcher.

were, "Now, Brother Fletcher, you are young and when you have a little more experience you will see the fallacy of this statement."[45]

Brimhall respected and encouraged women both as students and as teachers. Reaching out to women, he established the Brigham Young University Women's Organization in 1916. He "conceived the idea that such an organization, consisting of faculty wives and women teachers, could be of great help in looking to the welfare of the school, [and] in promoting sociability among faculty members," in turn adding to the university's success. Margaret Lawrence Eastmond was appointed to spearhead the organization.[46]

The president's influence on faculty and staff began with the hiring process. Brimhall was adamant about selecting teachers himself. Years later with respect to an assignment to "get teachers for ... the seminaries" he confided to his journal: "Application for position means nothing in selection of teachers. I want to select. I want to select."[47] If a prospective teacher were a member of the Church, an essential qualification Brimhall looked for was loyalty to and love for the restored gospel. An interaction with a Church member who was applying for a faculty position revealed Brimhall's insistence on faithfulness and orthodoxy. The applicant wrote to Brimhall, "From my conversations with you and your letters to me it is evident that I have given you the impression that I am out of sympathy with the Church and all that it stands for." The applicant continued, "While I concede that I have said and written things which would lead you to this conclusion, yet I surmise that you have looked me over suspiciously, as people do one who has been away to a University."[48]

Brimhall's reply was stinging: "I am of the impression that while you have sympathy with Mormons, you are out of sympathy with Mormonism." Answering the man's accusation that Brimhall was suspicious of him because of his university education, Brimhall declared, "Your inference that people who attend universities are generally looked upon with suspicion, seems to me to be just a little inappropriate."[49]

While loyalty to the Church was a priority for prospective teachers, it did not mean that only Church members could teach at BYU. Teacher Annie Pike Greenwood, who was not LDS, wrote about Brimhall, "Should he say 'Will you do this thing?' not one of us but what would strain every nerve to bring about the accomplishment of that which [Brimhall] desired or suggested and we not only did the thing, but we outdid ourselves, surprised ourselves with a best that we did not know we possessed."[50]

Hiring teachers was not easy. Offering them an adequate wage was a constant concern. Beginning in 1900, when he was acting president of BYA, Brimhall petitioned the General Church Board of Education to improve wages. At the time, among Church schools, BYA had the lowest salaries. To make things worse, teachers were only "paid one-third of their salaries in cash and the balance in scrip. Scrip was often discounted ten percent at local stores."[51] Brimhall declared, "It is positively humiliating to a member of our faculty to ask for more compensation." Since the faculty's salaries were low, Brimhall feared teachers would think their services were less important than other endeavors. He said, "I know that some of our teachers cannot meet their monthly living expenses without either borrowing or drawing on the[ir] savings." He continued to petition Church leaders "to set the pace in a most worthy economic policy."[52] A record of university salaries from the 1905–6 academic year to the 1908–9 academic year shows that some faculty salaries did rise by as much as $550. Brimhall's salary, however, did not change; it remained $2,352.[53]

Annie Pike Greenwood

Annie Pike was born in Provo, Utah, in 1879. Her father, a doctor who had emigrated from England, was the first superintendant of the Utah state mental hospital in Provo. Neither ever joined the LDS Church, but Annie attended and graduated from Brigham Young Academy and always sang its praises. In 1899 she wrote the words to the official "College Song," and in 1901, for Karl Maeser's funeral, she wrote a tribute that was included in LDS hymnals until 1985: "Come, lay his books and papers by, He shall not need them more; The ink shall dry upon his pen, So softly close the door. His tired head, with locks of white, And like the winter's sun Hath lain to peaceful rest tonight,—The teacher's work is done." This hymn was also sung at Brimhall's funeral in 1932. In 1925 she was given the BYU Alumni Association's Distinguished Service Award.

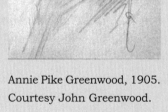

Annie Pike Greenwood, 1905.
Courtesy John Greenwood.

For a brief time she taught at the university with Brimhall and later wrote he "knew how to unlock the secret doors of our beings." In 1905 she married Charles Greenwood, who became a farmer in southern Idaho. In 1934, her book *We Sagebrush Folks* "won glowing reviews" in the New York newspapers. "An intimate, colorful portrayal of the daily life of the sagebrush farmers and their families, mercilessly truthful, but written with vivacity, cleverness, and humor," wrote Florence Finch Kelly in the *New York Times* Book Review. "Assuredly the country will hear more from Mrs. Greenwood—in fact, it may come to know her very well," echoed Caroline B. Sherman in the *New York Herald Tribune*. But the book did not sell well, perhaps because of the Great Depression. Annie continued to write but published little more. She passed away in Sacramento, California, in 1956.

Aldrich, Emily Hanks. "Cheer Anew for the BYU." *BYU Magazine* 61 (Fall 2007): 56.

Brigham Young University Alumni Association. Karl G. Maeser Funeral. February 19, 1901.

Daines, Gordon. "The Songs of BYU." *BYU History, L. Tom Perry Special Collection.* http://lib.byu.edu/sites/byuhistory/2009/02/26/the-songs-of-byu/.

Greenwood, Annie Pike. "The Teacher's Work Is Done." In *Hymns: The Church of Jesus Christ of Latter-day Saints*, no. 338. Salt Lake City, Deseret Book Company, 1974.

Greenwood, Annie Pike. *We Sagebrush Folks.* University of Idaho Press, Moscow, ID, 1988.

Groberg, Jennie H., and Delbert V. Groberg. *Biography Collection: George H. Brimhall.* N.p.: Alsina Elizabeth Brimhall Holbrook Family, 1988. Tributes, 106.

Ruckman, Jo Ann. Forword and afterword. In Annie Pike Greenwood, *We Sagebrush Folks,* xiv and 488. Moscow, ID: University of Idaho Press, 1988.

Wilkinson, Ernest L., ed. *Brigham Young University: The First One Hundred Years,* 4 vols. (Provo, Utah: Brigham Young University Press, 1975).

Brimhall reported to Church President—and president of the BYU Board of Trustees—Joseph F. Smith about "teachers who have so patriotically stood by the school, many of them at lower salaries than they could get elsewhere."[54] However, Brimhall warned Elder Richard R. Lyman that such devotion could not go on forever: "We are going to lose some very valuable men unless we can increase their salaries to the point of just a little more than a living." Although Brimhall hated the thought that some of the best faculty might leave the school over the low salaries, he acknowledged "[It may] be a good thing to have a general exodus of high class men from our school as perhaps it will be the only way to prove the falacy of the idea that education attracts the mediocre of people who cannot make a living any other way."[55]

Relationship with General Authorities and the Church Board of Education

During Brimhall's presidency, the BYU Board of Trustees helped to govern the university, but Brimhall relied more heavily on the General Church Board of Education, which governed all church schools, including BYU. He took a subordinate role to that board and sought its approval as he changed and implemented policy and curricula. Future BYU President Ernest Wilkinson said of this chain of command,

> During the years 1904 to 1908 the Church Board of Education, concerned about the rising costs of the Church school system, took a number of steps to control funds and to regulate courses of study. Academic programs, physical facilities, and even the organizational structure of the schools were modified. The board of examiners (composed of the three major Church school presidents and the Church superintendent), which had existed since Maeser's time, and a special committee of appropriations (composed of four or five members of the Council of the Twelve and the Church superintendent of schools), began to assume more responsibility for governing the Church school system.[56]

In a letter to Reed Smoot on March 8, 1911, Brimhall stated, "The school follows the Church or it ought to stop."[57] As

George H. Brimhall, ca. 1910. Courtesy L. Tom
Perry Special Collections.

president, he made it clear to faculty and students that
the General Church Board of Education, directed by the
priesthood leadership of the Church, had the final say in
all situations.[58]

In 1901, as acting president of BYA, Brimhall was sum-
moned to Salt Lake City for a special meeting with the General Church Board of Education in the office of Church
President Lorenzo Snow. A proposal to move all college work
to the University of Utah and cut education at BYA and other
church schools to elementary and high school levels was
presented to the board.[59] Brimhall favored keeping college

work at the Church schools. However, after a long discussion, President Snow said that he "favored the University of Utah if the Church could maintain control of it." Brimhall then forecasted, "We might get hold of the University, but we could not keep hold of it."[60] The meeting ended with no action taken. That night Brimhall made a terse entry in his journal, "Meeting of board of Education at Prest. office. Big discussion. Saved the College Dept. of B.Y.A, University tried to cut it out of existence."[61]

Brimhall as University President

In 1904 there were 1,275 students at BYU, but fewer than 60 were enrolled in the college division. The rest were elementary, intermediate, and high school students.[62] Once he became president, Brimhall focused much of his time and energy on the college division. He wrote to the board of trustees,

> High schools are coming into existence all around us and there is increased demand for college work. Our students, in the near future, will come from high schools seeking learning at the college level. It should therefore, be our policy to strengthen our college faculty and facilities to accommodate this growth.[63]

At the close of his first year as president, Brimhall reported that the university was "a school of seven schools," a structure he had largely inherited.[64] Under Brimhall, the college enrollment steadily increased, although levels hit a plateau and even decreased during the years of World War I.[65]

Brimhall believed that the mission of the Church was much larger than the school's mission and that only as a subordinate arm of the Church would the school achieve greatness. Although there were times during his administration when, due to the Church's financial problems, board members and others suggested BYU be closed, moved, or turned over to the state, Brimhall believed that as long as the school maintained a firm Church connection, it would survive and prosper.[66]

As president of the university, Brimhall took every opportunity to have as much personal association with members of the Church Board of Education as possible. He extended invitations to General Authorities to visit campus, meet with the students, and learn firsthand about the school. He gave the First Presidency and members of the Quorum of the Twelve Apostles campus tours, invited them to present summer school lectures, and asked the Church President to present diplomas to the graduates during commencement exercises.[67] When Brimhall became acting president of BYA in 1900, he invited President Lorenzo Snow to attend the school's annual handshake dance so students could shake a prophet's hand.[68]

Brimhall had an especially close relationship with Heber J. Grant. He stood firmly behind Elder Grant's constant request that Latter-day Saints keep the Word of Wisdom, even suggesting that a building be erected on the BYU campus named the "Word of Wisdom Memorial" and funded by getting students to contribute their "tobacco money."[69] Although Brimhall and Elder Grant shared similar goals for BYU, differences still arose.

On one occasion, Elder Grant opposed keeping a certain professor whom Brimhall favored retaining. Elder Grant acquiesced to Brimhall and, according to Brimhall's recollection, stated, "If that is the way you feel about it, I have no desire to press my side any further." Brimhall then wrote to Elder Grant in a style lost to future generations: "The tenderness with which you handled my feelings on that occasion sweetened, beyond expression, the strong attachments which had existed before." Brimhall said Elder Grant's "tone of voice [was] so full of sincerity and respect" that Brimhall felt "almost crushed" by it. He added, "I felt that I was being melted under the radiant ray of brotherly love." He ended the letter by testifying, "The nearer I get to my brethren, the more perfect they become to me."[70]

Years later, when dedicating the George H. Brimhall Building on the BYU campus, then Church President Heber J. Grant pronounced his personal benediction on his friend and their relationship: "George H. Brimhall was one of the choicest, finest, most spiritual-minded, loyal, true men that I ever knew. That sums it all up. I am very grateful for my personal and intimate acquaintance.... My association with Brother Brimhall was absolutely perfect."[71]

Brimhall's daughter Fawn married David O. McKay's brother Thomas E., so when Elder McKay visited campus, he stayed at the Brimhall home.[72] Still, Brimhall's correspondence with McKay illustrates the respectful relationship he maintained with all Church leaders. One example involved a letter from a faculty member who had written to Elder McKay complaining about the discontinuance of one of her courses. In turn, Elder McKay wrote Brimhall to set the teacher straight, assuring him that the faculty member was taking "a wrong view of this entire matter."[73] Brimhall responded to Elder McKay,

> [The teacher's] firmness borders on her obstinacy in not yielding to anything she does not recognize as authority, and at the same time her willingness to obey the decision of recognized authority puts her in the category of those whose humility guards very strongly against humiliation, and she is very tender on the latter point.

Brimhall's respectful relationship with Elder McKay and with Church leaders in general is expressed in the letter's conclusion: "Your explanations and statements concerning your attitude towards the department and the teacher is all-sufficient for me. I would have needed no explanation and no line of argument beyond your candid declaration."[74] Brimhall's correspondence regularly expressed his dedication and loyalty to the Church. He informed the Presiding Bishopric, "The motto of this school has always been, 'We follow the Church.'"[75]

Over the years, Church leaders reciprocated the loyalty Brimhall showed them. In 1907, after speaking at the university, Elder J. Golden Kimball of the Quorum of the Seventy said to Brimhall, "Surely you are blessed of the Lord and equipped for that great responsibility, and I pray the Lord to make you strong and vigorous physically, as well as mentally, and that you may be wrapped round about as with a garment with the spirit of the Lord."[76] In 1916, President Joseph F. Smith wrote to Brimhall, "We need you, Brother George. There is work for you to do of greater value than all earthly riches, and you posses richly the spirit of that work, and you have been endowed with gifts and wisdom which fit you for it in an unusual degree."[77]

A University of Religion

Brimhall saw himself as first and foremost a Church educator. He wanted LDS gospel principles to permeate every aspect of the university experience. He believed that if the institution followed gospel principles, it would have success and unity.[78] Brimhall declared, "In our amusements, our class work, our assemblies, our athletics, in everything, we will be governed by the directive force that is at the head of the Church trying to keep and interest us in the gospel principles."[79]

To aid in this endeavor, Brimhall emphasized religion courses. He believed religious education not only distinguished BYU but also gave it the advantage over all other institutions of higher learning. In a 1926 report to the General Church Board of Education, he wrote,

> The Brigham Young University holds an enviable position among the institutions of higher learning throughout the United States. Its departments of natural and mathematical sciences, commerce, history, music, art, and education all receive splendid recognition. But primarily it is a University of Religion.

He then explained:

> Religion has suffered tremendously as the result of efforts to identify it with theological dogma. But here, where every department and class is aiming toward building men and citizens; where in the art and music of man as well as in the handiwork of nature, we can read, plan, and design; where a sympathetic faculty is working with a pliant student body a glorious opportunity presents itself.
>
> At the B.Y.U. we see the agents of humanitarian interest working under their most favorable circumstances. And immediately we get a broader and more beautiful conception of what religion really is.[80]

Brimhall continued to work with a student mentoring program in which all students had a personal advisor from the theology faculty who would give them "special confidence, counsel, and guidance." Brimhall instructed these advisors to become "intimately acquainted with each student placed under his or her care."[81]

Missionary Class, 1912. Brimhall front row center. Courtesy L. Tom Perry Special Collections.

From early in his experience as a Church educator, Brimhall was interested in the training of missionaries. He felt that BYU was the ideal location for missionary training to take place. When the school was still an academy, he presented plans for missionary training classes to the board of trustees.[82] His recommendations were enacted, and missionaries continued to be trained at BYU during his tenure as president. The classes were well received by Church leaders. For example, German E. Ellsworth, president of the Northern States Mission, wrote to Brimhall, "We feel that the greatest thing that your school has done to the missionaries who have come to us is to help them to gain a testimony of the Gospel."[83] And Ben E. Rich, president of the Eastern States Mission, wrote to Brimhall, "There is little doubt that the missionary classes in the church schools are doing a great work."[84]

Expanded Offerings

Under Brimhall's leadership, the home economics department, instituted after Emma Lucy Gates donated "nearly one thousand dollars, with a view to founding . . . a domestic science department, bearing the name of her grandmother Lucy B. Young," was given a home on the top floor of the missionary and preparatory building completed in 1904. "To raise funds for this project," Gates (who later became a world-renowned opera star and the wife of future apostle Albert E. Bowen) had given musical recitals.[85]

Years later Zina Young Card corresponded with Brimhall and suggested she be hired to teach a short course to prepare the young women of the school for the "future duties that [would] rest upon them as wives and mothers." Card, who served on BYU's Board of Trustees, insisted she was being led by "the promptings of the Spirit."[86] A prominent scientist donated his private chemical laboratory for the chemistry courses.[87] An Aspen Grove summer school was established where nationally known educators lectured, and Leadership Week (forerunner of BYU's Education Week) and other community activities were instituted, which kept local citizens "involved and enthralled with their Church university."[88]

A Campus for the College

The landscape of the BYU campus changed dramatically during President Brimhall's administration. As acting president, he expanded the school by erecting a training building that included a men's gymnasium.[89] After he became president in 1904, the Missionary and Preparatory Building was completed as well as a blacksmithing building, made possible through the generosity of Jesse Knight.[90] In 1906 a recognizable feature of Utah Valley was painted—the block Y on the mountainside above the campus. Tradition

Preparing hot lime to whitewash the Y, ca. 1908. Courtesy L. Tom Perry Special Collections.

Whitewashing the Y, ca. 1911. Courtesy L. Tom Perry Special Collections.

Students working forges in the old blacksmithing shop, ca. 1904. Courtesy L. Tom Perry Special Collections.

holds that the initial plan was to paint the initials BYU on the mountainside. To center the letters correctly, students began working on the middle one first, but never proceded to the other letters after finishing it. Harvey Fletcher recalled his experience in creating the Y: "The students stood in a zig zag line about 8 feet apart stretching from the bottom of the hill to the site of the Y. The first man took the bag of lime, sand or rocks and carried it 8 feet and handed it to the second man." This procedure continued with all the students in the line, "each man shuttling back and forth along his 8 foot portion of the trail." The enthusiastic students had "expected to be through by 10 o'clock A.M. But it was a much bigger job than anyone expected. It was 4 P.M. before the Y was covered and then by only a thin layer [of whitewash]."[91]

The most notable landscape change during Brimhall's administration occurred when the university obtained land on a ridge northeast of the existing campus known as Temple

Procession to Temple Hill to dedicate land for a new campus, January 16, 1908. Courtesy L. Tom Perry Special Collections.

Hill. Brimhall and his contemporaries planned to build a college campus on the new land.[92] The idea for a new campus arose shortly after the name of the school was changed from Brigham Young Academy to Brigham Young University in October 1903, a few months before Brimhall became president. The thought was that the existing lower campus would continue to house the training, intermediate, and high school portions of the school, but the college students would eventually occupy new buildings on the new upper campus on Temple Hill. The land was known as Temple Hill because, according to tradition, Brigham Young had prophesied that a Church temple would be built there.[93] Although a temple had not been built there, Elder John Henry Smith said that fulfillment of the prophecy was "apparent in the prospect that a temple of learning ... shall crown this hill."[94] Church President Joseph F. Smith dedicated Temple Hill "for educational purposes" on January 16, 1908.[95]

Jesse Knight, member of BYU's board of trustees and generous financial benefactor to the university. Courtesy L. Tom Perry Special Collections.

Students and faculty posing to form a giant Y at the dedication of Temple Hill, January 16, 1908. Courtesy Groberg family.

Brimhall sought financial support for the campus expansion on Temple Hill from many sources. He asked the student body to give up their pleasure money. Students went without candy, gum, shows, and dances for three weeks and raised $1,049 to help purchase the land.[96] He also courted those who lived in the community. But, as in other fundraising efforts, his main support came from mining magnate Jesse Knight.

The Knight and Brimhall families were close neighbors and trusted friends. In 1899, Brimhall's oldest daughter, Jennie, married Knight's second son, Jesse William (Will).[97] When Brimhall was acting president of BYA in 1901, Knight became a member of the academy's board of trustees.[98] In

Jessie Knight

Jessie Knight was born in 1845 in Nauvoo, Illinois, the son of Newel K. and Lydia Goldthwaite Knight. His father died sixteen months later, leaving his mother with seven children to care for. From a young age, Jesse worked hard to support himself and help his family.

He married Amanda McEwan in 1869 and took up ranching near Payson, Utah. He also began to prospect and experienced small successes in locating and selling mining claims. However, during this time he distanced himself from the Church and often spoke against it. In 1887, his and Amanda's five children became desperately ill from drinking water from a poisoned well. Their two-year-old daughter, Jennie, was miraculously healed following a priesthood blessing from two LDS elders. A month later their oldest daughter, Minnie, 17, the only one of the children to have been baptized, quietly passed away. Jessie remembered that her last breath was a prayer: "Oh, God, bless our household." All of this triggered an intense soul searching in Jesse, who later recorded, "I prayed for forgiveness and help. My prayer was answered and I received a testimony." Thereafter, he dedicated his life to God.

In 1896 he struck a vein of ore in the Humbug mine that opened the way to financial success. Over time he built a mining, ranching, manufacturing, and banking empire that he considered to be a divine stewardship through which he should bless the lives of others and assist the Church. He developed a reputation for enlightened labor policies, honest business practices, and generous philanthropy. Between 1898 and his death in 1921, he donated over half a million dollars to BYU, earning him the title of "patron saint." He and Brimhall were close friends and neighbors. In 1910 Brimhall told the BYU student body, "I thank the lord for Brother Knight," a sentiment echoed by many others.

Knight, Jesse William. *The Jesse Knight Family: Jesse Knight, His Forbears and Family.* Salt Lake City: Deseret News Press, 1940.

Peterson, Richard H. "Jesse Knight, Utah's Mormon Mining Mogul." *Utah Historical Quarterly* 57 (Summer 1989): 240–53.

1905, Brimhall recorded that Knight sent an invitation to have a soda water with him. Brimhall wrote in his diary that day that Knight's quitting tobacco was a struggle. Brimhall wrote, "I have felt that I would like to put my hands on his head and bless him that he may not fail. The chief purpose of this effort is to put himself in a condition that he may have the spirit of the Lord to direct him in the use of his wealth."[99] The next year, Knight gave BYU five hundred acres of land on the Provo Bench to be sold as needed for revenues.[100] When Knight died the month before Brimhall was released as president of the university, Brimhall confided in his journal, "I've lost the presence of my strongest friend. How [Knight] would carry me through trouble. I seem now to be quite alone. He understood me."[101] Earlier in his journal, Brimhall had written of Knight, "He was more to mankind than they knew."[102]

With the financial help from the students and Jesse Knight, the land that Brimhall sought for campus expansion was secured. He then suggested to the board of trustees "that steps be taken to erect a new building to cost from $75,000.00 to $100,000.00." He felt the cost "could be met by appealing to the Alumni Association and to the friends and patrons of the institution."[103] The building would be known as the Karl G. Maeser Memorial and would represent "both the school's devotion to its past and its aspirations for the future."[104] The imposing classroom building with its Beaux Arts style, classical portico, and heavy white stone was to be the first structure on the new college campus, designed to include a quadrangle of academic buildings and a Church temple.[105]

The Maeser Memorial was completed in fall 1911 and dedicated on May 30, 1912,[106] but the financial burden on the faculty, administration, students, and friends of the school turned out to be greater than anyone had expected.

Cornerstone laying for the Maeser Memorial Building, October 16, 1909.
Courtesy L. Tom Perry Special Collections.

Brimhall said, "Some of us have paid what would mean
nearly a half year's salary."[107] By 1914 the obligations
incurred for the building had become a great liability for the
school. Its financial situation became desperate. Because of
the financial strain, unofficial reports circulated that BYU
would be closed or consolidated with another Church school
in Salt Lake City. The school's board of trustees met in June
1914 and ordered Brimhall to liquidate assets.[108] In October,
Knight came to Brimhall's rescue again with a valuable gift
of irrigation stock.[109] The building was finally financed at a
cost of $114,000[110] with the Knight and Holbrook families
bearing the core of the cost.[111] Brimhall's second daughter
had married Lafayette Holbrook's son, Lafayette H. Holbrook.

George H. Brimhall *(left)* with grandson Raymond Holbrook holding great-grandson Fay, BYU trustee Lafayette Holbrook, and son-in-law Lafayette Hinckley Holbrook at Raymond's Stanford Law graduation in 1931. Courtesy Groberg family.

Similar to Knight, Holbrook was on BYU's Board of Trustees. He had also previously served as mayor of Provo.[112]

After the Maeser Memorial was completed, Brimhall turned his attention to other aspects of campus infrastructure. In August 1912, he recommended to the board of trustees that a steel bridge or viaduct be constructed to connect the third floor of the Arts Building with the second floor of the High School building to lessen the need for young women to climb the stairs. In the same report, Brimhall also recommended the construction of a greenhouse for the Agricultural Department that was later completed at a cost of five hundred dollars.[113]

The most popular form of recreation during Brimhall's administration was dancing. Brimhall wanted to provide

BYU students with an amusement hall where they could have dances under proper supervision. In a recommendation to the board of trustees, he proposed

> that the University erect an amusement hall on its property on the west side of Academy Avenue between Fifth and Sixth North streets to cost approximately $12,500, and that the money be secured by borrowing it, using the 25,000 shares of Provo Reservoir Company stock as collateral security.

The board approved this proposal, later adding the provision that the building should also include a women's gymnasium. In 1913 the Women's Gymnasium was completed at a cost of about thirty thousand dollars.[114]

When funds for improvements were difficult to obtain, Brimhall would often solicit his faculty for "sweat equity." This occurred during summer 1914 when "the men's gymnasium needed a new floor, but the Church appropriation for the year's expenses" was deficient. Brimhall somehow secured the lumber without cost and then asked his faculty to lay a new floor. The faculty responded and spent two days of their summer vacation installing the new floor. Likewise, Brimhall solicited faculty and students to dig sewer trenches, build mountain trails, lay cement sidewalks, and complete other necessary improvements when funds were depleted.[115] However, none of these efforts were adequate to stem the tide of budget deficits that the school faced in the years after the completion of the Maeser Memorial building. As a result, plans to expand the college campus on the land adjoining the Maeser Memorial were shelved indefinitely.[116] The deficits continued to grow and crimped not only the campus expansion but the very operation of the school itself until in 1918, the First Presidency offered to assume all the school's liabilities in return for the school deeding all of its

Groundbreaking for the Women's Gymnasium, November 6, 1912. Courtesy L. Tom Perry Special Collections.

"The Fools' Frolic" in the Women's Gymnasium, 1920. Courtesy L. Tom Perry Special Collections.

Auto mechanics class in the Mechanic Arts Building, 1918. Courtesy L. Tom Perry Special Collections.

assets (mainly land) to the Church.[117] It was the end of an era for BYU and the beginning of another. Brimhall's often expressed belief that the school would prosper precisely because of its Church connections had been realized.

The entrance of the United States into World War I hastened the completion of the next building constructed on the proposed college campus: the Mechanic Arts Building. The school needed the building to accommodate regular growth, but Brimhall's desire to serve the war effort gave its completion added emphasis. Brimhall wrote Church and Board of Trustees President Joseph F. Smith proposing to make "preparation for military service an appendage to [the] physical education department."[118] Two days later, a letter was sent from the office of the First Presidency endorsing Brimhall's proposal.[119] In August 1918, Brimhall applied to the Church for an appropriation for the building and the Church budgeted $43,000 for its construction; but the war

Mechanic Arts Building. Courtesy Groberg family.

Dedication of the new Brimhall Building, October 16, 1935. Courtesy L. Tom Perry Special Collections.

ended before the building was completed.[120] After Brimhall's death, two stories were added to the Mechanic Arts Building and it was extensively remodeled into classrooms, labs, and offices. It was then dedicated on Founder's Day, October 16, 1935, by Church President Heber J. Grant as the George H. Brimhall building. The building has been extensively remodeled twice since then.[121] After the last remodeling, it was rededicated by Brimhall's great-grandson Elder John H. Groberg on August 11, 2005, at the request of the Church Board of Education.

World War I

The last few years of Brimhall's administration were marked by World War I and the ensuing influenza pandemic of 1918, both of which greatly affected BYU's enrollment and finances. During this time, many students and faculty left and could not be replaced. At one time, influenza

Assembly in College Hall at which students wore hygienic masks because of the influenza epidemic, ca. 1918. Courtesy L. Tom Perry Special Collections.

The Influenza Pandemic

The influenza pandemic of 1918–19 was one of the largest in history. The Spanish flu, as it was called, rapidly spread through the movement of troops during World War I. Half of the world's population had contracted the flu within a few months; over fifty million people died, more than double the number of casualties from the war. Unlike other influenza outbreaks, in which children and the elderly have been most at risk, this 1918 outbreak affected those in their prime—roughly half of the deaths occurred in people between age eighteen and forty. By November, the second wave of flu had passed, and the third wave, which occurred in 1919, had a smaller impact.

Everyday life was disrupted. The lack of healthy laborers caused industry, agriculture, and commerce to slow, and many cities began to resemble ghost towns as quarantines were enforced.

In Utah, so many people became sick that state officials began closing public gatherings and wearing masks became mandatory. The Church suspended meetings and closed the temples for months. Even Church President Joseph F. Smith, who died in November, did not have a public funeral. BYU closed from October 15, 1918 to January 1, 1919. Although the school closed, the military training program continued, and when the influenza raged through the Student Army Training Corps, none of the cadets died.

Phillips, Howard. "Influenza." In *The Oxford Encyclopedia of Modern World,* ed. Peter N. Stearns, 165-67. New York: Oxford University Press, 2008. Available online at http://www.oxfordreference.com/views/ENTRY.html?subview=Main&entry=t254.e769 (accessed February 17, 2009).

Tate, George S. "'The Great World of the Spirits of the Dead': Death, the Great War, and the 1918 Influenza Pandemic as Context for Doctrine and Covenants 138." *BYU Studies* 46, no. 1 (2007): 4–40.

Wilkinson, Earnest L. *Brigham Young University: The First One Hundred Years,* 1:453. 4 vols. Provo, Utah: Brigham Young University Press, 1975.

alone caused attendance to drop 50 percent. "Those in homes having influenza were quarantined in and those not having it were quarantined out."[122] Because of the pandemic, the institution closed from October 15, 1918, until January 1, 1919.[123]

After the United States entered World War I in April 1917, patriotic assemblies were held to encourage support for the war effort. Brimhall composed the words to a song to encourage students' patriotism:

> Old Glory wave on, o'er the land of the free,
> The home of the fair and the brave;
> The land where oppression from mountain to sea
> Finds only a place for a grave.
> The hands of a nation grasp firmly thy staff,
> In triumph they bear thee along;
> We join in the chorus like millions before us,
> Still pledging our banner in song.[124]

Music to the words was composed by Professor C. W. Reid.[125] The chorus paraphrased a religious hymn and gained great popularity:

> We'll come at the call of thy colors, Old Flag;
> We're ready for duty today.
> We'll serve where you want us to serve, Old Flag;
> We'll pay what you want us to pay.

Brimhall also penned the following lines:

> Now, while we stand on Freedom's soil,
> Inhaling Freedom's air,
> Be this the burden of our song,
> Our morn and evening prayer:
>
> O gracious Giver of our land,
> May we who in it live

Students preparing posters supporting the Third Liberty Loan campaign, ca. 1917. Students leant a hand to raise funds for the U.S. war effort during World War I. Courtesy L. Tom Perry Special Collections.

> Be grateful now for this best gift,
> The Grace of Power to Give.
>
> Great time, great place, great circumstance,
> To open wide the heart,
> To grow like Him who gave his all,
> By giving now our part.
>
> To fast betimes, with bread at hand,
> And feed the hungry throng,
> Of fragments make a plentitude,
> In sacrifice be strong.[126]

Many young men at the school enlisted in military service, including BYU's student body president Earl B. Snell.[127] Brimhall informed Church President Joseph F. Smith, "There is a demand here in the school for military training,

Utah and BYU during World War I

When Archduke Franz Ferdinand, heir of Austria-Hungary, and his wife were assassinated in Sarajevo in 1914, most Utahns could not have imagined they would become embroiled in the worldwide conflict that resulted. However, as the Great War continued, and American ships were in increasing danger of attack from German submarines, American leaders abandoned the policy of neutrality and joined the Allied forces in April 1917.

BYU and Utah County did not go untouched. Almost twenty-one thousand Utahns served in the war and 665 died, most due to illness. Women served as nurses, ambulance drivers, and canteen workers. By October 1917, sixty-five young men from Utah County left for basic training before being deployed to France. Sixteen BYU students gave their lives in service to their country.

Utahns who remained at home worked to further the war effort by planting gardens, volunteering in agricultural work, preserving food, donating money, going without meat and sugar, and making socks and afghans for soldiers. BYU held patriotic assemblies, and students raised almost ten thousand dollars for Liberty Bonds and the YMCA War Fund. The school curriculum was rearranged as administrators began incorporating army training, and students were able to attend with government funding.

Powell, Allan Kent. "World War I and Utah." *Utah History to Go.* http:// historytogo.utah.gov/utah_chapters/from_war_to_war/world-war1andutah.html (accessed March 4, 2009).

Wilkinson, Ernest L. *Brigham Young University: The First One Hundred Years,* 1:445–454, 602. 4 vols. Provo, Utah: Brigham Young University Press, 1975.

"World War I." *Encyclopedia Britannica.* 2009. http://search.eb.com/ eb/article-9110198 (accessed March 4, 2009).

Student Army Training Corps standing at "post arms" on the steps of the Maeser Building, 1918. Courtesy L. Tom Perry Special Collections.

and unless we supply that demand, a number of our boys will undoubtedly leave school to get this training."[128] The First Presidency approved Brimhall's request and "the University sent three faculty members to the Presidio in San Francisco, California, to qualify as military instructors." BYU officially opened its Army Training Corps Center on October 1, 1918.[129]

During Brimhall's administration, a new college campus was begun and new buildings and programs were constructed and implemented. However, his primary concern was that the school should build people—students, staff, and faculty—so that they could, in turn, build Zion. He believed the BYU faculty and its graduates would be great assets to the Church. In 1914 he wrote to the Presiding Bishopric of the Church, "I think I can say with perfect safety that the faculty of the Brigham Young University will hold up the hands of the authorities of the Church ... in the teaching and training of the people of this dispensation."[130] As president, Brimhall strived to model noble and Christ-like principles for the faculty, who in turn were to do the same for the students. Brimhall realized his leadership and actions set the tone for the university. He showed patience and concern for BYU employees, and his management style involved more counseling than commanding.

Notes

Epigraph quoted from "My Desire," in Jennie H. Groberg and Delbert V. Groberg, *Poetry* (n.p.: Alsina Elizabeth Brimhall Holbrook, [1988]), 132; set to music by Florence Jepperson Madsen in 1938.

1. George H. Brimhall, *Diary of George H. Brimhall,* 2 vols. (n.p.: Alsina Elizabeth Brimhall Holbrook Family, [1990]), 1:178, September 3, 1898.

2. Brimhall, *Diary,* 1:190, January 3–4, 1899.

3. George H. Brimhall to Orson F. Whitney, January 15, 1924, Brimhall Presidential Papers; underlining in original.

4. George H. Brimhall, "Health Problems, and Testimony of Administrations to Sick," in Groberg and Groberg, *Biography Collection,* 75. Later, Brimhall blamed himself for these health problems, attributing them to "unwise overwork." George H. Brimhall to "My Dear Student Friends," May 8, 1920, in Groberg and Groberg, *Biography Collection,* 31.

5. Brimhall, *Diary,* 1:298, February 17, 1902; Holbrook and Holbrook, *Tall Pine Tree,* 76–78.

6. Holbrook and Holbrook, *Tall Pine Tree,* 78.

7. Brimhall, *Diary,* 1:314, January 5, 1903.

8. See, for example, Brimhall, *Diary,* 1:315, January 8, 1903.

9. Brimhall, *Diary,* 1:319, February 4, 1903.

10. Holbrook and Holbrook, *Tall Pine Tree,* 78.

11. Poulsen, oral history interview, 10.

12. George H. Brimhall to Alice Grover, December 17, 1928, in *Tributes,* 137.

13. George H. Brimhall, *Poetry* (n.p.: Alsina Elizabeth Brimhall Holbrook, [1988]), preface.

14. This poem is included in the unpublished Alsina Elizabeth Brimhall Holbrook collection of Brimhall's works in a volume titled "Poetry," page 158¾ in the possession of Joseph H. Groberg.

15. Holbrook and Holbrook, *Tall Pine Tree,* 78.

16. Brimhall, *Diary,* 1:305, August 1–9, 1902; 1:308, October 16–17, 1902; 1:331, April 22, 1903.

17. Mark H. Brimhall, "An Account of the Year My Father Was with Me on My Mission in California, during His Illness," in *Tributes,* 348; ellipsis in original.

18. Holbrook and Holbrook, *Tall Pine Tree,* 80.

19. See Diane L. Mangum, "The First Sister Missionaries," *Ensign* 20 (July 1980): 62.

20. Family group sheet, in Groberg and Groberg, *Biography Collection,* [324]; "Flora Robertson Brimhall," in Groberg and Groberg, *Biography Collection,* 304.

21. Holbrook and Holbrook, *Tall Pine Tree,* 80.

22. "Notes on His Health," in Groberg and Groberg, *Biography Collection,* 74, taken from an account written by Mark H. Brimhall, February 1957. Apparently Brimhall was first asked to serve as acting president and one year later became president.

23. Ernest L. Wilkinson, ed., *Brigham Young University: The First One Hundred Years,* 4 vols. (Provo, Utah: Brigham Young University Press, 1975), 1:382.

24. Brimhall, "Called as BYU Acting President," 1:35–36.

25. Wilkinson, *First One Hundred Years,* 1:382.

26. "Notes on His Health," in Groberg and Groberg, *Biography Collection,* 72–73.

27. "Report of the Presidency of the Brigham Young University for the Twenty-Eighth Academic Year, Ending May 26, 1904," George H. Brimhall Presidential Papers, L. Tom Perry Special Collections, Harold B. Lee Library, Brigham Young University, Provo, Utah.

28. Benjamin Cluff, Diary, Summary for 1903, Perry Special Collections; Benjamin Cluff to Frank Warren Smith, 18 August 1897, Frank Warren Smith Papers, Perry Special Collections.

29. J. Gordon Daines III, email message to author, April 24, 2008. As Brigham Young University archivist, Daines sent the following figures, which show an increase in population: 386 (1892); 825 (1903); 1,275 (1904); 1,449 (1906); 1,553 (1907); 1,600 (1923). "Prior to Franklin S. Harris the bulk of students were high school or elementary students. Most of the growth of the college population prior to Wilkinson occurs under Harris." Furthermore, records show that "in 1912 the university graduated its first four-year-graduating class with eighteen members." Ernest L. Wilkinson, ed. *Brigham Young University: The First One Hundred Years,* 4 vols. (Provo, Utah: Brigham Young University Press, 1975), 4:404. But by 1923, 670 of the 1,600 students were college students. Daines, email message to author, April 24, 2008.

30. Brigham Young University, Board of Trustees records, April 16, 1904, Perry Special Collections.

31. Wilkinson, *First One Hundred Years,* 1:584.

32. Clinton David Christensen, "Joseph Brigham Keeler: The Master's Builder" (master's thesis, Brigham Young University, 1997), 172.

33. Wilkinson, *First One Hundred Years,* 1:582.

34. Wilkinson, *First One Hundred Years,* 1:512.

35. Merrill taught education and agriculture. Wilkinson, *First One Hundred Years,* 1:514, 585.

36. See, for example, "Brigham Young Academy," *Deseret Evening News,* July 27, 1888, [2].

37. Wilkinson, *First One Hundred Years,* 1:382–83.

38. According to Wilkinson, "Joseph B. Keeler became responsible for financial matters, while Edwin S. Hinckley frequently worked with the faculty." Wilkinson, *First One Hundred Years,* 1:465. Wilkinson further elaborated, "During the closing years of Brimhall's administration, he was physically so incapacitated with heart trouble that, in order to preside over the student body assemblies held in old College Hall, he was carried up the stairs by Ed Hinckley, one of his counselors, through a back stairway so that he could not be seen." "Highlights in the Ninety-Nine-Year History of BYU," 254. See also Wilkinson and Skousen, *School of*

Destiny, 183–184; and Wilkinson, *First One Hundred Years,* 1:493, 582. However, this story seems unlikely as Edwin S. Hinckley was released as a counselor to Brimhall in 1915 and moved to Ogden six years before the end of Brimhall's administration. It is possible that something like Wilkinson's account occurred near the beginning of Brimhall's administration before Brimhall fully recovered his health. When Edwin S. Hinckley passed away in 1929, Brimhall wrote a poem entitled "The Passing of E. S. Hinckley," which does refer to his help when Brimhall "was weak and ill." A portion of the poem follows:

> It bowed my head, slowed my step,
> The world grew strangely dim;
> I wondered why they did not call
> For me instead of him.
> Him, whom I loved, had leaned upon
> When I was weak and ill,
> Struck down by death in prime of life
> And left me living still.

Jennie Holbrook Groberg and Delbert V. Groberg, *Poetry* (n.p.: Alsina Elizabeth Brimhall Holbrook, [1988]), 17. A slightly different version of this poem appears in Raymond Brimhall Holbrook and Esther Hamilton Holbrook, *The Tall Pine Tree: The Life and Work of George H. Brimhall* (n.p.: By the authors, 1988), 145–46.

39. Ernest L. Wilkinson, "Highlights in the Ninety-Nine-Year History of BYU," in *Speeches of the Year: BYU Devotional and Ten-Stake Fireside Addresses, 1974* (Provo, Utah: Brigham Young University Press, 1975), 255–56; Brimhall, *Diary,* 1:370, April 11, 1905; Ernest L. Wilkinson and W. Cleon Skousen, *Brigham Young University: A School of Destiny* (Provo, Utah: Brigham Young University Press, 1976), 183–84.

40. George H. Brimhall, "What Was He?" in Reinhard Maeser, *Karl G. Maeser: A Biography by His Son* (Provo, Utah: Brigham Young University, 1928), 162–63. See also Alice Louise Reynolds, "Biographical Sketch of George H. Brimhall," in George H. Brimhall, *Long and Short Range Arrows,* comp. and ed. Harrison R. Merrill

and Alice L. Reynolds (Provo, Utah: Brigham Young University Press, [1988]), 9.

41. George H. Brimhall, "Benjamin Cluff," May 17, 1904, in George H. Brimhall, *BYU Devotional Talks,* 2 vols. (n.p.: Alsina Elizabeth Brimhall Holbrook Family, [1988]), 1:38.

42. George H. Brimhall, Baccalaureate address, May 26, 1901, in George H. Brimhall, *Longer Talks* (n.p.: Alsina Elizabeth Brimhall Holbrook Family, [1988]), 11.

43. George H. Brimhall to Susa Giles, June 8, 1906, Brimhall Presidential Papers.

44. George H. Brimhall to Joseph F. Merrill, April 29, 1915, Brimhall Presidential Papers.

45. Harvey Fletcher, "History of Harvey Fletcher," typescript, 26–27, Perry Special Collections.

46. J. Marinus Jensen, N. I. Butt, Elsie C. Carroll, and Bertha Roberts, "History of Brigham Young University," unpublished manuscript, 55–56, Perry Special Collections; T. Earl Pardoe, *Sons of Brigham* (Provo, Utah: Alumni Association, 1969), 310.

47. Brimhall, *Diary,* 2:893, August 10, 1922.

48. A. L. Neff to George H. Brimhall, April 1, 1906, Brimhall Presidential Papers.

49. George H. Brimhall to A. L. Neff, April 4, 1906, Brimhall Presidential Papers.

50. Annie Pike Greenwood, in *Tributes to George H. Brimhall* (n.p.: Alsina Elizabeth Brimhall Holbrook Family, [1988]), 106. See also Jeffrey R. Holland and Patricia T. Holland, "A Faithful Friend Is a Strong Defense," in *Speeches of the Year: Brigham Young University, 1982–83* (Provo, Utah: Brigham Young University, 1983), 10–11.

51. Wilkinson, *First One Hundred Years,* 1:346.

52. George H. Brimhall to Adam S. Bennion, November 15, 1919, Brimhall Presidential Papers; underlining in original.

53. Wilkinson, *First One Hundred Years,* 1:494n58.

54. George H. Brimhall to Joseph F. Smith, January 2, 1917, Brimhall Presidential Papers.

55. George H. Brimhall to Richard R. Lyman, March 18, 1920, Brimhall Presidential Papers.

56. Wilkinson, *First One Hundred Years,* 1:392.

57. Wilkinson and Skousen, *School of Destiny,* 212n47.

58. George H. Brimhall, "Loyalty," March 16, 1911, in Brimhall, *BYU Devotional Talks,* 1:278.

59. Wilkinson, *First One Hundred Years,* 1:361–64.

60. Wilkinson, *First One Hundred Years,* 1:361–64.

61. Brimhall, *Diary,* 1:272, June 25, 1901.

62. Wilkinson and Skousen, *School of Destiny,* 187–88.

63. Quoted in Holbrook and Holbrook, *Tall Pine Tree,* 86.

64. "Report of the Presidency of the Brigham Young University for the Twenty-Eighth Academic Year," 2–3.

65. See Daines, email message to author, April 24, 2008.

66. George H. Brimhall, "BYU, a Church Institution," April 26, 1905, in Brimhall, *BYU Devotional Talks,* 1:82. See also George H. Brimhall to Reed Smoot, March 8, 1911, Brimhall Presidential Papers; Wilkinson and Skousen, *School of Destiny,* 212n47.

67. See, for example, Brimhall, *Diary,* 2:806, April 5, 1917; and George H. Brimhall to Joseph F. Smith, May 19, 1913, Brimhall Presidential Papers.

68. George H. Brimhall to Lorenzo Snow, December 7, 1900, cited in Groberg and Groberg, *Biography Collection,* 79.

69. George H. Brimhall to Heber J. Grant, February 10, 1920, Brimhall Presidential Papers.

70. George H. Brimhall to Heber J. Grant, December 7, 1916, Brimhall Presidential Papers.

71. Heber J. Grant, "Address by President Heber J. Grant: Dedication Brimhall Bldg.," October 16, 1935, in *Tributes,* 28.

72. Brimhall, *Diary,* 1:521, November 15, 1908.

73. David O. McKay to George H. Brimhall, February 19, 1914, Brimhall Presidential Papers.

74. George H. Brimhall to David O. McKay, April 24, 1914, Brimhall Presidential Papers.

75. George H. Brimhall to the Presiding Bishopric, May 15, 1914, Brimhall Presidential Papers.

76. J. G. Kimball to George H. Brimhall, September 19, 1907, Brimhall Presidential Papers.

77. Joseph F. Smith to George H. Brimhall, January 3, 1916, in *Tributes,* 2.

78. George H. Brimhall, "Privileges and Rights," February 5, 1907, in Brimhall, *BYU Devotional Talks,* 1:154.

79. George H. Brimhall, "BYU, a Church Institution," April 26, 1905, in Brimhall, *BYU Devotional Talks,* 1:82.

80. George H. Brimhall, "The Place of Seminaries and a Church University in Modern Education," in Brimhall, *Longer Talks,* 135.

81. "Report of the Presidency of the Brigham Young University for the Twenty-eighth Academic Year," 3.

82. Holbrook and Holbrook, *Tall Pine Tree,* 75.

83. German E. Ellsworth to George H. Brimhall, September 22, 1910, Brimhall Presidential Papers.

84. Ben E. Rich to George H. Brimhall, August 24, 1910, Brimhall Presidential Papers.

85. Jensen and others, "History of Brigham Young University," 47–48; *Brigham Young University Quarterly: Church Teachers College Annual Catalogue for the School Year 1913–1914* 8, no. 3 (February 1, 1913), 14. Emma Lucy Gates was the daughter of Susa Young Gates. See p. 198.

86. Zina Young Card to George H. Brimhall, October 18, 1919, Brimhall Presidential Papers. See also Zina Young Card to George H. Brimhall, November 20, 1919, Brimhall Presidential Papers.

87. George H. Brimhall to James E. Talmage, September 11, 1918, Brimhall Presidential Papers.

88. Ruth Roberts Lusk, "Personal Recollections of President George H. Brimhall," as excerpted in Groberg and Groberg, *Biography Collection,* 246.

89. Wilkinson, *First One Hundred Years,* 3:482.

90. Wilkinson, *First One Hundred Years,* 1:385–86.

91. Fletcher, "History of Harvey Fletcher," 15–16.

92. Wilkinson, *First One Hundred Years,* 1:405nn10–11. See also 1:452 regarding the erection of the Mechanic Arts Building on the hill in 1918.

93. Wilkinson, *First One Hundred Years,* 1:405n9.

94. "Remarks of Elder John Henry Smith on the Occasion of the Dedication of Temple Hill, January 16, 1908," *White and Blue* 25, no. 1 (October 24, 1911): 11.

95. *Brigham Young University Quarterly: Annual Catalogue for the School Year 1915–1916* 10, no. 4 (May 1, 1915): 18.

96. Brimhall, *Diary,* 1:454, December 13, 1907; George H. Brimhall and Marion Harris to "Our dear Friend of the B.Y.U.," December 13, 1916, cited in Groberg and Groberg, *Biography Collection,* 141.

97. Family group sheet, in Groberg and Groberg, *Biography Collection,* [324].

98. Wilkinson, *First One Hundred Years,* 1:358.

99. Brimhall, *Diary,* 1:371, April 13, 1905.

100. "Excerpts from Minutes of Meetings of the Board of Trustees of the Brigham Young University, Which Related to a Gift from Jesse Knight and Family, of Five Hundred Acres of Land on Provo Bench," Brimhall Presidential Papers.

101. "Diary of George H. Brimhall: 1881–1932," typescript, 1949, 397, March 18, 1921, Perry Special Collections. In some references to this journal entry, the words "rain and snow" appear at the end of the last sentence. However, these words most likely referred to the weather on the day of the journal entry.

102. "Diary of George H. Brimhall," 397, March 16, 1921.

103. "Excerpts from the Minutes of the Meetings of the Board of Trustees of the Brigham Young University Relating to the Maeser Memorial Building," Brimhall Presidential Papers.

104. Wilkinson and Skousen, *School of Destiny,* 192. See also Wilkinson, *First One Hundred Years,* 1:507.

105. Wilkinson, *First One Hundred Years,* 1:405n10–11.

106. Brimhall, *Diary,* 2:627, May 30, 1912.

107. George H. Brimhall to Annie Ronnow, January 19, 1911, Brimhall Presidential Papers.

108. Wilkinson, *First One Hundred Years,* 1:442–43.

109. Wilkinson, *First One Hundred Years,* 1:443; "A Gift of Nearly $250,000 for B.Y.U.," *Provo Herald,* September 24, 1914, 1.

110. George H. Brimhall and Marion Harris to "Our Dear Friends of the B.Y.U.," December 13, 1916, in Groberg and Groberg,

Biography Collection, 141; Wilkinson, *First One Hundred Years,* 1:405.

111. Wilkinson, *First One Hundred Years,* 1:408n14. The list of contributors in this book incorrectly identifies the Holbrooks as members of the Jesse Knight family. See also Brimhall and Harris to "Our Dear Friends," December 13, 1916.

112. Groberg and Groberg, *Biography Collection,* 57.

113. Jensen and others, "History of Brigham Young University," 109.

114. Jensen and others, "History of Brigham Young University," 110–11.

115. Jensen and others, "History of Brigham Young University," 54–55.

116. Wilkinson, *First One Hundred Years,* 1:435–38.

117. Wilkinson, *First One Hundred Years,* 1:445.

118. George H. Brimhall to Joseph F. Smith, April 2, 1917, Brimhall Presidential Papers.

119. Joseph F. Smith, Anthon H. Lund, and Charles W. Penrose to George H. Brimhall, Joseph B. Keeler, and Amos N. Merrill, April 4, 1917, Brimhall Presidential Papers.

120. Wilkinson, *First One Hundred Years,* 1:451–52.

121. "George H. Brimhall Building Rededication," program, August 11, 2005, Perry Special Collections; Wilkinson, *First One Hundred Years,* 2:231.

122. Holbrook and Holbrook, *Tall Pine Tree,* 80.

123. Wilkinson says the school was closed from October 15, 1918, to January 1, 1919, but that the army training continued until the Armistice was signed in November. See Wilkinson, *First One Hundred Years,* [1]: [445–54].

124. George H. Brimhall, "Old Glory," *Improvement Era* 20 (July 1917): 795.

125. Jensen and others, "History of Brigham Young University," 57.

126. George H. Brimhall, "The Grace of Power to Give," *Improvement Era* 21 (March 1918): 406.

127. Jensen and others, "History of Brigham Young University," 57.

128. Brimhall to Smith, April 2, 1917.

129. Smith, Lund, and Penrose to Brimhall, Keeler, and Merrill, April 4, 1917; Wilkinson, *First One Hundred Years*, 1:449.

130. Brimhall to the Presiding Bishopric, May 15, 1914.

"The aim of my existence is
To seek the truth, apply it well
And in my work be glad;
Be much more moved by love of good
Than by the fear of bad."

George H. Brimhall, 1913

6

Brimhall Confronts Modernism

As a professional educator, Brimhall stayed informed of national education trends. He read books, attended professional conventions, and visited well-known schools in the eastern United States. Although he believed BYU was mostly on par with other schools, he still wanted to raise the institution's academic status, so he decided to hire more faculty members with graduate degrees from leading universities. The decision became a double-edged sword. It brought in well-trained scholars, but it also brought in the ideas of modern biblical criticism and scientific inquiry that often were in tension, if not at complete odds, with fundamental Latter-day Saint beliefs. One episode became polarizing, and its resolution shaped the way religion was taught at BYU. This controversy deeply affected Brimhall personally. He was fiercely loyal to Church authorities and Church doctrine, but he also had great confidence in the principles of scientific inquiry. Moreover, he explicitly trusted his faculty to uphold the doctrines and principles of the gospel within

165

William James

The elder brother of novelist Henry James, William James was an influential American philosopher, psychologist, and educator. William's interests were broad. In addition to his studies in chemistry, comparative anatomy, and medicine at Harvard University, William studied art in Paris and the United States. He interrupted his medical training for a zoological expedition to Brazil and a research trip to Germany to study physiological psychology. After completing his medical degree, William taught anatomy, physiology, and later psychology at Harvard.

In 1890, William published *The Principles of Psychology*, a comprehensive study of nineteenth-century psychology. In this work, he coined the term "stream of consciousness." His work in philosophy became recognized when he published *Pragmatism* in 1907.

Beyond his influence in the fields of philosophy and psychology, William was an educator who believed in the Socratic method. He made his students comfortable expressing their ideas.

William believed that truth was not abstract but that it was practical, verifiable by human experience. He also was concerned with religious and moral ideas. In some ways, all of his philosophical writing represented an intellectual search for faith. Although he did not subscribe to any particular religion, he believed the physical world was part of a larger spiritual universe and that when a man connected to this spiritual realm, his life became richer and more meaningful.

Allen, Gay Wilson. "James, William." In *Encyclopedia Americana.* Available online at Grolier Online, http://ea.grolier.com/cgi-bin/article?assetid=0220840-00 (accessed January 27, 2009).

Haack, Susan. "Pragmatism." In *Encyclopedia Americana.* Available online at Grolier Online, http://ea.grolier.com/cgi-bin/article?assetid=0320590-00 (accessed January 28, 2009).

Madsen, Truman G. "William James: Philosopher-Educator." *BYU Studies* 4, no. 1 (1961): 81–105.

their academic lessons and, by disposition, tended to be patient with them. He believed that "no fair study of science or philosophy could jeopardize the faith of a thinking student." He was especially confident of this at BYU, where, he believed, each department contributed "to the department of religious education."[1]

Pedagogy Pioneers

Brimhall received all his formal education at BYU. Nevertheless, he was very interested in the ideas of his generation's pedagogical pioneers. He lectured on "Parker's principles on Unity of Idea"; shared the wisdom of psychologist and philosopher William James; discussed formative and informative education; defined the pedagogical philosophies of several modern educators;[2] and, like Cluff before him, invited philosopher, psychologist, and educational reformer John Dewey to lecture in Provo.[3]

During his trips to California and the eastern United States, Brimhall visited high schools, colleges and universities, including the Parker School in Chicago, the Horace Mann School in Boston, the University of Chicago and its laboratory school, the University of California in Berkeley, Stanford University in Palo Alto, and Columbia University in New York City.[4] Based on these visits, he concluded that BYU did not suffer in comparison.[5] He said,

> We are very strong on the initiative. They do not sing their own songs to the extent that we do. They do not paint their own pictures. They do not have the atmosphere of correlation. I wish to emphasize that right here that so far as atmosphere, and actual appearance of correlation is concerned, I will be safe in saying without any fear of contradiction that we are superior.[6]

John Dewey

John Dewey was one of the most influential American thinkers of his time. His ideas impacted the fields of philosophy, psychology, education, law, and political science. His philosophy focused on the practical application of ideas, particularly in how instrumental these ideas were in solving problems. Dewey believed experimentation and the scientific method were the best ways to find solutions to social and ethical difficulties.

Dewey graduated from the University of Vermont in 1879; he earned a PhD from Johns Hopkins University five years later. During his career, he taught philosophy, psychology, and pedagogy at the University of Michigan, the University of Minnesota, the University of Chicago, and Columbia University.

Educational reform, however, was Dewey's main interest. Traditional teaching methods focused on the subject matter, and students were expected to learn through memorization. Dewey felt teaching should be more student-centered than subject-centered and that teachers should build instruction based around students' interests. Dewey also advocated laboratory classes and workshops where students could interact and experiment. In his view, teachers were counselors who would help students develop not just academically but as a whole person.

Some felt his ideas decreased the quality of education because some teachers took his ideas too far and neglected essential subjects in favor of entertaining students. Regardless of differing opinions, Dewey is arguably the best-known educator in American history.

Brickman, William W. "John Dewey." In *Encyclopedia Americana*. Available online at Grolier Online, http://ea.grolier.com/cgi-bin/article?assetid=0125920-00 (accessed March 9, 2009).

"John Dewey." In *Encyclopedia Britannica*. Available online at http://search.eb.com/eb/article-9030186 (accessed March 9, 2009).

Detail of George H. Brimhall *(left)*, John C. Swenson *(center)*, and John Dewey *(right)*, 1901. Brimhall invited Dewey, a famous philosopher, psychologist, and educational reformer, to lecture at the summer school. Courtesy L. Tom Perry Special Collections.

Brimhall read voraciously to keep abreast of new ideas that could benefit BYU. After one educational conference, for example, he recorded his desire to purchase the following books: *The Proofs of Life after Death* by Robert J. Thompson; *On the Trail the Immigrant* by Edward A. Steiner; *Vocational Education* by Covley (which he noted was free); *The Twentieth Century New Testament*, and *The Fleming*.[7] Brimhall was also an active participant in the Utah Educational Association (UEA) and the National Education Association (NEA). He attended conventions from New York City to San Francisco,[8] where he was exposed not only to different educational ideas, but also to the practices of different religious traditions. While being respectful of other religions, Brimhall still filtered them according to his own beliefs. At a convention in Los Angeles, for example, a Jewish rabbi opened the proceedings with prayer. Brimhall recorded, "The rabbi's prayer was full of open-eyed instruction to Divinity, elequent and orderly but lacking in every respect the essentials of an inspired petition."[9]

New BYU Faculty

In 1907, Brimhall hired two brothers: Joseph Peterson, who held a PhD in psychology from the University of Chicago and was the first PhD employed at BYU, and Henry Peterson, who held degrees from the University of Chicago and Harvard University. The next year, Brimhall hired Ralph Chamberlin, with a PhD from Cornell, and in 1909, he hired Ralph's brother William Chamberlin; although William did not hold a doctoral degree, he had studied at Harvard, the University of California, the University of Chicago, and the University of Utah. Joseph Peterson oversaw the psychology department. Henry Peterson, a member of the Church's Sunday School General Board, helped oversee the College of Education. Ralph Chamberlin took charge of the biology department, and William Chamberlin taught psychology, philosophy, and languages. All four were active Latter-day Saints and were enthusiastic about teaching at a Church-owned school. They took an interest in the students and invigorated the campus with the spirit of scientific inquiry.[10]

Initially, Brimhall was pleased with the exciting new atmosphere. It appears he was not concerned that these new professors were teaching organic evolution. He even appointed the Peterson brothers and William Chamberlin as part-time theology faculty.[11] However, it soon became apparent that some of their students were questioning fundamental Church teachings. One of the students, Annie Clark Tanner, recorded, "One of my greatest disturbances occurred when I learned that the story of Adam and Eve and the Garden of Eden may not be literally true. Its literal acceptance had been one of the important premises in Mormonism." She continued,

> If the story of the flood came from legends of a people
> the Israelites had met in captivity, or if the Book
> of Jonah was a satire of Jewish self-righteousness
> and written as a fable to portray that characteristic
> rather than as history, why accept literally the story
> of the Creation as related in the *Bible*?[12]

Such doubts soon culminated in a campus crisis.

Although this incident is often called "BYU's evolution controversy," the crisis actually stemmed more from the teaching of higher criticism of the Bible, in which scientific theories were used to explain the development of theological beliefs. As historian Richard Sherlock explains, "Ostensibly the source of the controversy was the teaching of evolution, but the crucial issue was … the broader question of scholarly endeavor and religious interpretation."[13] The new teachers began to have a large following on campus that led to heated discussions between those who sided with the new professors and those who disagreed with their views. Reports of these conflicts reached Church headquarters from as far away as Mexico and were referred to Brimhall's administrative superior, Horace Hall Cummings, the super-intendent of Church schools.[14]

Brimhall believed the faculty members could work out these differences among themselves. In December 1910, he wrote President Joseph F. Smith,

> As they look at it their teachings are in perfect har-mony with the principles of the Gospel, but there are certainly many who cannot perceive that har-mony, and, therefore it seems to me that a little waiting with their working will be in keeping with greater wisdom on their part.[15]

Cummings, however, was determined to bring the matter to a head. In his autobiography, Cummings recalled that after some students told Brimhall "they had quit praying, as they had learned in the school that there was no real God to hear them," Brimhall began to worry.[16] Cummings wrote that Brimhall had a dream, which he interpreted to be a direct warning.

> [Brimhall] saw several of the B.Y.U. professors standing around a peculiar machine on the cam-pus. When one of them touched a spring a baited fish hook attached to a long thin wire rose rapidly into the air....
>
> Casting his eyes around the sky he discov-ered a flock of snow-white birds circling around the clouds and desporting themselves in the sky, seemingly very happy. Presently one of them, seeing the bait on the hook darted toward it and grabbed

George H. Brimhall and wife Flora *(couple on the right)* at an excavation of dinosaur bones, ca. 1920s. Courtesy Groberg family.

it. Instantly one of the proffessors on the ground touched a spring in the machine, and the bird was rapidly hauled down to the earth.

On reaching the ground the bird proved to be a B.Y.U. student, clad in an ancient Greek costume, and was directed to join a group of other students who had been brought down in a similar manner. Bro. Brimhall walked over to them, and noticing that all of them looked very sad, discouraged and downcast, he asked them:

"Why, students, what on earth makes you so sad and down-hearted?"

"Alas, we can never fly again!" they replied with a sigh and a sad shake of the head.

Their Greek phylosophy had tied them to the earth. They could believe only what they could demonstrate in the laboratory. Their prayers could go no

higher then the ceiling. They could see no heaven—
no hereafter.[17]

According to Cummings, this dream deeply impacted
Brimhall and was a turning point in his handling of the
controversy.

The Cummings Report

Cummings visited BYU in November and December 1910
for about nine days before reporting to Church leaders. One
review of Cummings's report explained that it stated "the
positive as well as [the] negative effects the new learning
seemed to have on students." The same reviewer noted that,
in a positive light, Cummings had reported that many on
campus had successfully reconciled LDS doctrine and modernism, increased their class attendance, and participated
in stimulating, good-natured discussion. In addition, Cummings believed most students had not lost faith.[18] However,
Cummings also noted,

> There seems to be a struggle still going on between
> their new views and their old ones, and at times,
> their words are full of light and at other times and
> on the same subjects they would be full of dark-
> ness. The struggle that both teachers and pupils
> describe[d] to me as having taken place in their own
> hearts when the new thought was being presented
> to them, was very fierce, and often robbed them of
> appetite and sleep.[19]

In January 1911, Cummings sent his report to the General Church Board of Education. It outlined his observations
about "the nature and effect of certain theological instructions" being taught at BYU. He claimed the following con-
cepts were taught at the school: "The flood was only a local

inundation of unusual extent"; "the confusion of tongues came about by the scattering of the families descended from Noah when they became too numerous for the valley they originally occupied"; "winds blew the waters of the Red Sea"; "Christ's temptation is only an allegory of what takes place in each of our souls"; "there is no personal devil to tempt us"; "John the Revelator was not translated"; "ordinances may be helpful props to weak mortals"; "all truths change"; "visions and revelations are mental suggestions." Cummings also stated, "The objective reality of the presence of the Father and the Son, in Joseph Smith's first vision, is questioned." Cummings concluded, "Faith now seems to be regarded with pity, as superstition, and is not a characteristic of the intellectually trained."[20]

He declared that these teachers were "among the strongest and best educated men in the faculty," and they "converted many of the other teachers and most of the students, to their views."[21] One week after the report was released, Cummings summarized it before the BYU faculty. Brimhall aligned himself with Cummings. In response, teacher Amos Merrill called for a faculty committee to investigate the veracity of the Cummings report. According to one historian, Brimhall asked his faculty to keep criticism of university administration and the General Church Board of Education in the background and to remain loyal to the university.[22] Nevertheless, it soon became clear that the General Church Board of Education, composed of the Church's leadership, was concerned and wanted action to be taken.[23]

Brimhall's Response

Once he understood the position of Church leaders on this matter, Brimhall acted quickly. "I recognize now that a more vigorous course of action on my part might have been better," he wrote to his friend Elder Reed Smoot, "but I was lenient,

Reed Smoot

Reed Smoot was a close friend and confidant of George H. Brimhall. Smoot was born January 10, 1862, in Salt Lake City, but moved to Provo with his family in 1872. He attended Brigham Young Academy's first class in 1876 and graduated with the class of 1880. Smoot served on the school's board of trustees from 1893 to 1938. He married Alpha M. Eldredge in 1884 and in 1890, as a married man, left on a mission to England. As part of the mission, he and BYA classmate James E. Talmage toured Europe in 1891. Smoot returned home that same year. On April 8, 1900, he was called to the Quorum of the Twelve Apostles, where he served until his death in 1941.

In 1902 he received permission from Church President Joseph F. Smith to run for the United States Senate. His election led to a four-year battle to see if he would be allowed to serve in that body because of his Church calling. Perhaps no event had a greater influence on the Church's public image than those long hearings at which even President Smith was called to testify. They lasted until 1907 when, against the recommendation of the committee that conducted the hearings, the full Senate voted to seat Smoot. Over time he became one of the Senate's most influential leaders and even was featured on the cover of *Time* on April 8, 1929. However, he was defeated

Senator Reed Smoot was featured on the April 8, 1929, cover of *Time* magazine.

and patiently hopeful that men would change gradually as they have in other cases, but the storm, instead of dying out, increased in its fury." Brimhall continued by telling Smoot, "I would rather the Maeser Memorial remain a sealed tomb containing our college hopes and ambitions ... than to have its doors thrown open to influences antagonistic to the heroism, inspiration and revelation of those who have made the school."[24]

The General Church Board of Education minutes reveal Brimhall's course of action:

[Brimhall] expressed himself to the effect that the only thing that he could see to do was get rid of these teachers. He had patiently labored with them in the hope that they would change their attitude and abstain from thrusting their objectionable views before the classes but it seemed that they were more determined than ever to teach theology according to their own ideas and theories, instead of according to the revealed truth, and he therefore saw no alternative but to dispense with their services.[25]

A special committee made up of six Apostles, Brimhall, and Cummings, met with the Peterson brothers and Ralph Chamberlin. During a five-hour meeting, the three teachers defended their belief in higher criticism of the Bible and apparently "balked at recognizing the authority of the university president or Board of Trustees to rule on questions of science."[26] "[Ralph] Chamberlin and the Petersons believed that when scripture and science conflicted on certain points, scripture must give way to science."[27] After deliberating, the committee agreed the teachers would either need to conform to the committee's instructions or leave the university.[28] When Brimhall pleaded with the professors to change their curriculum, Chamberlin responded, "I never gave a public lecture on evolution until I had consulted you as to whether it would be all right. You urged me to do it. . . . Now, why have you changed suddenly?"[29]

Joseph Peterson and Ralph Chamberlin left the university voluntarily. Henry Peterson was dismissed.[30] Having to carry out this forced removal was heart-wrenching for Brimhall. He wrote a letter of termination to Henry Peterson and sent a copy to Church President Joseph F. Smith adding these words: "This is the first time during our administration that we have had occasion to handle a teacher, and the necessity is very, very painful to us."[31]

William Chamberlin, who had not been asked to meet with the committee, resigned from BYU in 1916. Beginning in 1913, most of his well-attended religion courses were cancelled. He later taught at the University of Utah and the Brigham Young College in Logan until 1921, when he was again invited to teach theology at BYU. However, he was in such poor health that he could not accept the offer. He died that same year.[32]

When news of the departures and dismissals spread across campus, students circulated a petition against the decision.[33] Among those who signed were Carl F. Eyring, B. F. Larsen, and Hyrum Manwaring.[34] On March 16, 1911, Brimhall spoke to the student body and faculty, comparing this crisis with the Mormon exodus. He described the suffering of the early Mormon pioneers who had fled Nauvoo, Illinois, in winter 1846. He said there was murmuring and that some chose not to go west. Those who did follow Church leaders circled their wagons against the wind and cold. "The fugitives sheltered by those ... wagons and tents were the people of whom we are the children," Brimhall said to those assembled. He added, "I ask you, my beloved students, not to give evidence to the world that you have lost faith in the leaders of Israel." He explained:

> If President Joseph F. Smith wants my counsel, he gets it. If the Board wants my advice, they get it; but I am not going to advise my board through avenues that are antagonistic to the institution that built the school.... I would rather my name be written on a tombstone than to see it in any array that could be justly construed to class me against my people; and when I say against my people, I say against the Priesthood of God, that I have learned to follow and not to oppose. Oh, it is hard to stand still; but it is harder to keep still and see the salvation of the Lord.
>
> Now in spite of all that may be said or done, the authorities of this school and of the Church School System will decide its policies; and those who work under the head know there is no power to judge the policy of the school, except those who preside over it. If there be a student or a teacher who recognizes any other directive source than that provided by the

Church, they may appeal to that source; but before anyone does this, in good conscience, in good form, I suggest that before you assume the right to dictate, that you retire from our banquet.[35]

Aftermath

A cloud of gloom descended over campus. For the next few months, Brimhall worked hard to improve morale. He wrote Elder Smoot in May, "I would be in perfect misery if I were not in harmony with those over me,—I can stand it to be out of harmony with others."[36] One of those with whom he was out of harmony, at least for this moment, was part-time BYU instructor Juliaetta Bateman Jensen, who wrote in her journal,

All of the faculty members who taught college courses, 1913. Brimhall seated in front center. Courtesy L. Tom Perry Special Collections.

> This fight has been extremely bitter in many ways. President B. [Brimhall] has talked to his faculty in the most insulting, uncultured manner such as no truly educated president would do to his faculty many of whom are far, far superior to him in scholarship, and in everything else. I have lost all my respect for him.... If the school is not injured I shall miss my guess.[37]

Another person who criticized the situation was prominent Utah educator Milton Bennion. In the *Utah Educational Review,* Bennion suggested that those who asked the professors to leave were confusing "essentials and non-essentials in faith."[38]

As soon as emotions stabilized, Brimhall tried to find replacement faculty members. He wrote Dr. Harvey Fletcher, a young physicist studying under Robert Millikan at the University of Chicago. Brimhall said, "If Harvey was my own son I would write him to come home." Fletcher agreed to come to BYU.[39]

Despite Brimhall's efforts, some believed the professional status of the faculty did not recover until the 1920s. Thomas L. Martin, BYU Dean of Applied Sciences, observed,

> We lost much when the Chamberlains [*sic*] and the Petersons left us. If some of the narrowness which caused the upheaval in 1911 could have been prevented from exercising its power, I believe the vision that George H. Brimhall had in mind would have been accomplished; and if we could have had a free hand with these men and their associates, people would be singing our praises.[40]

In hindsight, perhaps Brimhall could have managed this episode differently. Some believe that had he been willing to exercise more authority at the beginning of the episode, or even after Cummings's report, the situation may have ended better.[41] Certainly the experience was very hard on Brimhall personally. He knew he had done the right thing both for the school and for his conscience. Yet the outcome was unsettling. "There must be a reconciliation between science and religion which will not jeopardize the existence of either," Brimhall wrote later. He believed BYU was "the ideal place" for this reconciliation to take place and that in fact, that was its mission.[42] However, obeying Church leaders and defending his religious beliefs were hallmarks of his personality. Brimhall was consistently loyal and sensitive to the General Church Board of Education and to the leaders of the Church. In this episode, his two great causes—his religion and education—seemed to collide. He wanted the most qualified teachers at BYU; but even more importantly, he wanted the school to follow the leadership of the presiding authorities of the Church. For Brimhall, the former was desirable, but the latter was essential.

This incident had both positive and negative effects on the school. Brimhall's actions had exhibited his "complete loyalty to Church leaders [and] won the school acceptance in the eyes of the presiding authorities of the Church."[43] Even in the midst of the controversy, Brimhall perceived this positive result. He explained to Elder Smoot,

> The going of these professors will perhaps disturb the college and interfere with its immediate growth. They will have a following, but like the Church, in a short time the school will not only retrieve its lossess, but out of the accident [incident?] God will bring glory to the institution until it will be said, "It is a good thing it happened." There are some people who predict the death of the college

if these men go. I am ready to say that if the life of the college depends upon any number of men out of harmony with the brethren who preside over the Church, then it is time for the college to die.... The school follows the Church, or it ought to stop.[44]

Years later, on January 8, 1956, Church President David O. McKay dedicated a chapel in Brigham City for students of the Intermountain Indian School. Elder Boyd K. Packer, who accompanied President McKay as the supervisor of Church seminaries and institutes, was present that day. Elder Packer tells the story:

A very old man, a stranger to me, came forward on the arm of his daughter. He had come some distance to speak to President McKay. It was impossible for me not to hear their conversation. He gave President McKay his name and said that many years ago he had taught at BYU. President McKay said, "Yes, I know who you are." Tears came as the old man spoke sorrowfully about the burden he had carried for years. President McKay was very tender in consoling him. "I know your heart," he said. That old man was one of the three professors who had been hired by President Brimhall in 1910.[45]

After leaving BYU, Joseph Peterson taught psychology at the Universty of Utah until 1915. He later taught at the University of Minnesota and eventually at George Peabody College for teachers in Nashville, Tennessee. He became president of the American Psychological Association in 1934. He died in 1935.[46] Henry Peterson became superintendent of schools in Box Elder County, Utah, and in Logan Utah, and eventually professor and head of the department of education and psychology at Utah State University. He died in

1957.[47] Ralph Chamberlin taught at the University of Utah and at Harvard University until becoming professor of zoology at the University of Utah, from which he retired in 1938. He was the author of *The University of Utah: The First Hundred Years* published in 1960. He died in 1967.[48]

Although BYU lost three key faculty members in 1911, others were hired who also enhanced education at the university. After 1911, Harvey Fletcher guided students in the physical sciences. Carl F. Eyring joined the faculty in 1915 and later became dean of the College of Arts and Sciences. Eugene L. Roberts, who in 1910 accepted Brimhall's invitation to be the school's athletic coach and physical education chair, established athletic and outdoor traditions for the school and began the BYU Invitational Track Meet in 1911. Other faculty hired in 1911 and 1912 included Beatrice Camp (elocution and physical education), A. B. Christensen (history) and William Ward (mathematics).[49]

Church President Joseph F. Smith died in November 1918. Brimhall's presidency at BYU had roughly paralleled Joseph F. Smith's administration in the Church. Brimhall revered President Smith and viewed the BYU students and faculty—both LDS and non-LDS alike—as part of President Smith's own family. Brimhall told them, "I have never doubted that man, never."[50]

In July 1919, the administration of the Church Educational System was reorganized and Brimhall was asked to supervise the seminary program and to appoint a faculty executive committee to help him administer the university.[51] Brimhall gave vigorous leadership to the seminary program and helped develop excellent teachers.[52] Seminary teacher Russel B. Swensen recalled Brimhall sitting "in [Swensen's] classroom all day, waving his hand, asking and answering questions." Brimhall's first comments to Swensen were critical, and he considered the president to be a "very dogmatic and a very fierce man because [he] had seen him many times bawl out students who were talking in assembly." But then Brimhall encouraged Swensen, telling him, "I think you'll make a great teacher if you make some progress. You have the potential to be a great teacher."[53] Swensen went on to attend the Divinity School at the University of Chicago and then returned to BYU as a faculty member in the 1930s teaching religion and language courses.[54]

Notes

Epigraph quoted from a longer poem, "Why I Am," first published in the *Improvement Era* 17 (November 1913): 15, but which evolved over time. See, for example, "Heeding Counsel," *Relief Society Magazine* (March 1923). In a letter to Alsina Holbrook, February 2, 1927, in Jennie H. Groberg and Delbert V. Groberg, *Poetry* (n.p.: Alsina Elizabeth Brimhall Holbrook, [1988]), 62, Brimhall called these words "The best thing I ever wrote."

1. "The Place of Seminaries and a Church University in Modern Education," in George H. Brimhall, *Longer Talks* (n.p.: Alsina Elizabeth Brimhall Holbrook Family, [1988]), 134, 146.

2. See, for example, George H. Brimhall, *Diary of George H. Brimhall,* 2 vols. (n.p.: Alsina Elizabeth Brimhall Holbrook Family, [1990]), 1:110, November 16, 1893; 1:215, July 25, 1899; 1:200, March 16, 1899; and George H. Brimhall, "Ethics of the Doctrine and Covenants," *Young Woman's Journal* 10 (October 1917): 587.

3. Brimhall, *Diary,* 2:676, 685–86, June 22–July 2, 1914.

4. Brimhall, *Diary,* 2:674, February 20, 1914; 2:676, March 9–11, 1914; 2:713, March 1, 1915; 1:347, March 9–13, 1905; 1:426, March 1, 1907.

5. George H. Brimhall to Reed Smoot, March 12, 1915, George H. Brimhall Presidential Papers, L. Tom Perry Special Collections, Harold B. Lee Library, Brigham Young University, Provo, Utah.

6. "Report to the School: BYU Is Superior," March 26, 1914, in George H. Brimhall, *BYU Devotional Talks,* 2 vols. (n.p.: Alsina Elizabeth Brimhall Holbrook Family, 1988), 1:319.

7. Brimhall, *Diary*, 2:687, July 11, 1914.

8. Brimhall, *Diary*, 1:439, July 10, 1907; Raymond Brimhall Holbrook and Esther Hamilton Holbrook, *The Tall Pine Tree: The Life and Work of George H. Brimhall* (n.p.: By the authors, 1988), 86–87.

9. Brimhall, *Diary*, 1:483, July 1907.

10. Gary James Bergera and Ronald Priddis, *Brigham Young University: A House of Faith* (Salt Lake City: Signature Books, 1985), 134–35.

11. Bergera and Priddis, *House of Faith*, 135. In this account, Henry Peterson claimed that at one meeting Brimhall said, "I too am an evolutionist."

12. Annie Clark Tanner, *A Mormon Mother: An Autobiography* (Salt Lake City: Deseret News, 1941), 187–88; italics in original. Notwithstanding these doubts, Annie Clark Tanner reported that she enjoyed the classes (216–17).

13. Richard Sherlock, "Campus in Crisis: BYU, 1911," *Sunstone* 4, no. 1 (January–February 1979): 11.

14. Gary James Bergera, "The 1911 Evolution Controversy at Brigham Young University," in *The Search for Harmony: Essays on Science and Mormonism*, ed. Gene A. Sessions and Craig J. Oberg (Salt Lake City: Signature Books, 1993), 24–25.

15. George H. Brimhall to Joseph F. Smith, December 3, 1910, Brimhall Presidential Papers.

16. Horace H. Cummings, Autobiography, typescript, ch. 41, p. 6, Perry Special Collections.

17. Cummings, Autobiography, ch. 41, p. 6. See Ernest L. Wilkinson, ed., *Brigham Young University: The First One Hundred Years*, 4 vols. (Provo, Utah: Brigham Young University Press, 1975), 1:421–22, which adds the note that Brimhall did not mention the dream in any of his records.

18. Tim S. Reid, "Mormons and Evolution: A History of B. H. Roberts and His Attempt to Reconcile Science and Religion" (PhD diss., Oregon State University, 1997), 118; see also Sherlock, "Campus in Crisis," 13–14.

19. Reid, "Mormons and Evolution," 119.

20. Horace H. Cummings, "Written Report of His Investigations of the Theological Teaching in the College Department of the Brigham Young University," January 21, 1911, Uncategorized Church General Board of Education Minute Book, January 28, 1903–November 27, 1918, 182–83, Church History Library; as reprinted in Sherlock, "Campus in Crisis," 12, 13.

21. Cummings, Autobiography, ch. 41, p. 2.

22. BYU Faculty Minutes, January 28, 1911, cited in Bergera, "1911 Evolution Controversy," 29.

23. Wilkinson, *First One Hundred Years,* 1:424.

24. George H. Brimhall to Reed Smoot, March 8, 1911, Brimhall Presidential Papers.

25. General Board Minutes, February 3, 1911, in Wilkinson, *First One Hundred Years,* 1:424.

26. Bergera, "1911 Evolution Controversy," 29.

27. Reid, "Mormons and Evolution," 123.

28. Bergera, "1911 Evolution Controversy," 29.

29. Ralph V. Chamberlin, oral history interview, early 1963, typescript, 8, Perry Special Collections. According to Ralph Chamberlin, Brimhall answered, "Well, I'll tell you, Brother Chamberlin, I know which side my bread's buttered on."

30. Ralph V. Chamberlin, *Life and Philosophy of W. H. Chamberlin* (Salt Lake City: Deseret News Press, 1926), 159–160, 209–11; Bergera and Priddis, *House of Faith,* 143. See also, Wilkinson, *First One Hundred Years,* 1:428n63; Bergera, "1911 Evolution Controversy", 30–34.

31. George H. Brimhall to Joseph F. Smith, March 17, 1911, Brimhall Presidential Papers.

32. Chamberlin, *Life and Philosophy,* 148–52.

33. Chamberlin, *Life and Philosophy,* 148–52, gives a complete copy of the petition. Copies reprinted in "B.Y.U. Students Destroy Reply of Presidency and Make Public the Protest They Formulated," *Salt Lake Tribune,* March 16, 1911, 1, 3; and "Petition of Students Causes Much Alarm," *Provo Herald,* March 17, 1911, 1, list ninety-four signatures. The *Tribune* reported that there were only 125 students in the college division of the school.

34. Bergera and Priddis, *House of Faith,* 143.

35. George H. Brimhall, "Loyalty," March 16, 1911, in Brimhall, *BYU Devotional Talks,* 1:277–78.

36. George H. Brimhall to Reed Smoot, May 11, 1911, Brimhall Presidential Papers.

37. Juliaetta Bateman Jenson, Journal, about May 25, 1911, cited in Mark K. Allen, *The History of Psychology at Brigham Young University* (Provo, Utah: Psychology Department, Brigham Young University, 1975), 72.

38. Milton Bennion, "The 'Evolution' and 'Higher Criticism' Controversy at Brigham Young University," *Utah Educational Review* 4 (March 1911): 10.

39. Wilkinson, *First One Hundred Years,* 1:433, 438–39.

40. Thomas L. Martin to Heber C. Snell, March 16, 1942, Heber C. Snell Papers, Archives and Manuscripts, Merrill-Cazier Library, Utah State University, Logan, Utah.

41. Wilkinson, *First One Hundred Years,* 1:432.

42. George H. Brimhall, "The Place of Seminaries," in Brimhall, *Longer Talks,* 136.

43. Wilkinson, *First One Hundred Years,* 1:519.

44. Brimhall to Smoot, March 8, 1911.

45. Packer, "The Snow-White Birds," Brigham Young University Annual University Conference address, August 29, 1995, reprinted in John W. Welch and Don E. Norton, eds., *Educating Zion* (Provo, Utah: BYU Studies, 1996), 186. Actually, the professors in question were hired between 1907 and 1909.

46. Gary James Bergera, "The 1911 Evolution Controversy at Brigham Young University," in Gene A. Sessions and Craig J. Oberg, eds., *The Search for Harmony: Essays on Science and Mormonism* (Salt Lake City: Signature Books, 1993), 35.

47. Henry Peterson Papers (1893–1957), coll mss 105, Manuscript Register Biographical Note, Special Collections and Archives, Utah State University Libraries, Logan, Utah, available online at http://library.usu.edu/Specol/manuscript/collms105.html (accessed April 14, 2010).

48. Ralph Vary Chamberlin Papers Encoded Archival Description, J. Willard Marriot Library Special Collections, University of Utah, Salt Lake City, http://db3-sql.staff.library.utah.edu/lucene/Manuscripts/null/Accn0907.xml/Bioghist (accessed April 14, 2010).

49. See "Carl F. Eyring and BYU," *BYU History, L. Tom Perry Special Collections,* http://lib.byu.edu/sites/byuhistory/2010/06/09/carl-f-eyring-and-byu/ (accessed June 12, 2010); "Eugene L. Roberts, Athletic Pioneer," *BYU History, L. Tom Perry Special Collections,* http://lib.byu.edu/sites/byuhistory/2009/09/02/eugene-l-roberts-athletic-pioneer/ (accessed June 12, 2010); and Wilkinson, *First One Hundred Years,* 1:433.

50. George H. Brimhall, "Joseph F. Smith," April 20, 1905, in Brimhall, *BYU Devotional Talks,* 1:75, 78.

51. Wilkinson, *First One Hundred Years,* 1:454–57.

52. The exact nature of Brimhall's administrative responsibility for the Church's seminaries is not clear. According to Wilkinson, Brimhall was very active in this assignment but he also cites William E. Berrett as saying his administrative position was "mostly honorary." Wilkinson, *First One Hundred Years,* 2:104n38.

53. Russel B. Swensen, oral history interview, September 13, 1978, typescript, 8, Perry Special Collections.

54. Wilkinson, *First One Hundred Years,* 2:267, 282–83.

"I'm glad I've loved fair science;
I'm glad I've loved good art;
I'm glad I've loved religion
And held it to my heart.

I'm glad I've loved my fellowmen;
I'm glad I've loved my God;
I'm glad I've loved to fly on thought;
I'm glad I've loved to plod."

                 George H. Brimhall, 1928

7

The End of an Era

In April 1921, the General Church Board of Education announced Brimhall's release as BYU president, which would be made effective on July 1. Brimhall had served as acting president for two years and as president for seventeen. Church President Heber J. Grant said,

> I appreciate more than I can tell the very wonderful force and power and spirit of the Gospel of Jesus Christ that has been manifest in this school under the administration of President George H. Brimhall. I feel in my heart that from the time Brother Brimhall took charge of this institution, the spirituality in it, the spirituality that should characterize our school system, namely—that which is necessary for the making of Latter-day Saints—has existed in the school as perfectly as it is given of mortal man to make it.[1]

George H. Brimhall in his 1922 Dodge. Courtesy Groberg family.

Franklin S. Harris, a former student of Brimhall's, replaced him as university president, and Brimhall was named president emeritus and director of theology at BYU along with his ongoing responsibility as seminary supervisor.[2] He was sixty-eight years old and felt a great sense of accomplishment from his time at the university. He recorded, "I feel like the man who has driven his automobile to the brow of the hill and is now turning the wheel over to his son."[3]

Brimhall maintained an office on campus for the next eleven years. "From early morning until late afternoon each school day, his door was wide open."[4] He counseled students and spoke at university devotionals. At the same time, he allowed Franklin S. Harris to have complete autonomy. Happy with his new position, Brimhall wrote Harris, "My cup of BYU joy has simply been over-flowing ever since you took charge. I am working at what I like, with those I love, and under a leadership in which I have perfect confidence. What more is there to wish for than just a continuance?"[5]

Brimhall continued to deliver his trademark four-minute sermonettes at the school's weekly devotionals. In 1934 the university published a collection of these sermonettes in a book called *Long and Short Range Arrows*. It included sermonettes with such titles as "The Abundant Life," "As a Man Thrills," "Be Bravely Beautiful," "Building from Within," "The Church of My Choice," "Joseph Smith," and "Keep Up Your Correspondence with Your Father in Heaven."[6] It was listening to these weekly sermonettes given by the school's

Former President George H. Brimhall *(front row, far right)* with President Franklin S. Harris *(next to Brimhall)* and the College of Fine Arts and Sciences faculty, 1928. After his release, Brimhall continued to fulfill various duties at the school for many years. Courtesy L. Tom Perry Special Collections.

The Young Women's Mutual Improvement Association

Originally conceived as part of the women's Retrenchment Association formed by Brigham Young in 1869, the Young Ladies' Mutual Improvement Association was formed to help the young women of the Church grow spiritually and refrain from every form of worldliness in dress, speech, and manner. Early members even had a set attire they wore to help them avoid worldly trends in fashion. During the next few years, every ward in the Church formed a branch of the organization. The groups met weekly for gospel discussions, service projects, public speaking classes, and a mild exercise program, which featured ball bouncing, knee bends, side stretches, and croquet.

Shortly after the Young Men's Mutual Improvement Association was formed in 1875, the name of the young ladies' organization was changed to match, that is, Young Ladies' Mutual Improvement Association (YLMIA). The young men and young women soon began meeting together periodically. The YLMIA began developing lesson manuals and guides for its weekly meetings, and the group adopted a camping program.

In 1934 the name was changed to the Young Women's Mutual Improvement Association. The YWMIA had programs and classes designed to help girls develop skills in music, dance, and the performing arts. Eventually, the YWMIA came to resemble the modern Young Women's organization, splitting its members into groups according to age and interests and adopting themes, mottos, and symbols for each class. Although the organization changed over the years, its purpose has remained constant—helping young women grow in faith and building their testimonies.

Cannon, Elaine Anderson. "Young Women." In *Encyclopedia of Mormonism,* ed. Daniel H. Ludlow, 4:1616–19. 4 vols. New York: Macmillan, 1992.

president emeritus that later prompted Church President Ezra Taft Benson to say of his college years at BYU, "No man has so inspired me with so few spoken words as has President Brimhall."[7]

Auxiliary Work

Brimhall continued to serve the various auxiliary organizations of the Church. He wrote, spoke, counseled, and worked on the board of the Young Men's Mutual Improvement Association (YMMIA) until his death. He wrote "more lessons for [that organization] than any other person," completing his last lessons in 1931, the year before he died.[8] He also worked with the Young Ladies' Mutual Improvement Association (YLMIA). After he spoke to her board in 1931, YLMIA President Clarissa A. Beesley wrote to thank him for his presentation:

> Some want us to give up altogether, our manuals. Some want us to put more spirituality in our work and some think we are stressing the doctrinal too much; but you seem always to know just how to harmonize the entire scheme, you never "knock," you always give us encouragement.[9]

From 1921 to 1929, Brimhall also wrote theology lessons for the Relief Society. He wanted the women of the Church to develop into "thinking believers" and informed women that it pleased God for them to study.[10] Brimhall's theology lessons met the society's objectives, and Relief Society General Secretary Amy Brown Lyman told him, "Wherever Relief Society lessons are discussed, the women invariably report that the theology lessons are their first choice."[11]

Along with writing lessons, Brimhall edited lessons written by others. In the role of editor, he was demanding, yet kind and encouraging. In a 1904 letter to Susa Young

Susa Young Gates

The daughter of Brigham Young and Lucy Bigelow, Susa Young Gates was a prominent writer, editor, and women's activist in Utah. She began studying shorthand at age twelve and became so proficient that she became her father's personal secretary. Her first experience in publishing came at age fourteen when she became the editor of the newspaper at the University of Deseret, which she had been attending for a year.

Susa married Alma Dunford when she was sixteen; their marriage lasted only five years, ending in divorce in 1877. A year later, Susa entered Brigham Young Academy. There, she founded the music department and taught classes in domestic science. On a trip to the Sandwich Islands (Hawaii), Susa became reacquainted with Jacob Gates. They married in 1880.

Throughout her life, Susa stayed busy. She founded the *Young Women's Journal* and was its editor for forty years. She also edited the *Relief Society Magazine*. In addition to editing, Susa was a prolific writer of novels, biographies, histories, and genealogical works. She held positions on both the Relief Society and the Young Women's general boards and served on the boards of trustees of Utah State Agricultural College and Brigham Young Academy. Susa represented Utah multiple times at the National Council of Women and was chosen as the delegate from the United States to the International Council of Women in 1901. An activist in the woman's suffrage movement, Susa was a friend of Susan B. Anthony.

Plummer, Louise. "Gates, Susa Young." In *Encyclopedia of Mormonism,* ed. Daniel H. Ludlow, 2:535–36. 4 vols. New York: Macmillan, 1992.

Wilkinson, Ernest L. *Brigham Young University: The First One Hundred Years,* 2:767–68. 4 vols. Provo, Utah: Brigham Young University Press, 1975.

Susa Young Gates, photo taken by C. R. Savage. Courtesy
L. Tom Perry Special Collections.

Gates regarding a lesson she had submitted, Brimhall wrote,
"I have looked over your lesson on Habit, and have come to
the conclusion that while in the main it contains some most
valuable character building ideas, I feel that in its present
state it will not do you justice.... If it is not presumptuous

[I] shall be pleased to express some of my ideas." He then said that in its present form the lesson would "be seriously misunderstood" but encouraged Gates,

> I am sure that you want nothing but the latest and best to go from you as the product of your pen. Please now don't worry about this as I wish to assure you that there is in your paper the foundation for something of the greatest value to the young people for whom it is intended.[12]

Brimhall's wife Flora reported that "night after night [her husband] sat up outlining yearly theology programs for the auxiliary organizations.... He put his whole soul into these projects, regarding each one in the light of a mission call."[13] Diary entries such as, "About home working on M.I.A. lessons," and, "Worked all day on Relief Society Lessons," were typical of the years Brimhall spent writing Church lessons.[14] Church President Heber J. Grant wrote Brimhall during this time:

> I wish to say to you that I am very, very grateful for the splendid work that you have been doing for the Era in writing lessons for the Senior Classes. I have not read them all but nearly all and I have never read one but what I have been impressed with the inspiration and splendid spirit that has guided you in writing these lessons....
>
> I know of no single worker from the time that the M.I. Associations were first organized until today, who has put more genuine thought and study and has done more work for the advancement of our young men than your own dear self.
>
> I am wondering, my dear brother, if you ... have been guilty of over-doing.[15]

But Brimhall had a hard time slowing down.

In March 1926, the Church's leadership was again in the throes of evaluating the economic sustainability of its educational programs. At issue was not only the objectives and priorities of Church education, but the very existence of a Church university that had to compete with tax-supported institutions.[16] The Church Board of Education asked Brimhall to present his ideas on the "function and possibilities" of the Church's schools and seminaries at a special board meeting in the office of the First Presidency.[17] The letter from superintendent of Church education Adam S. Bennion invited Brimhall to give "to the brethren the benefit of your long experience." Brimhall's principal work at the time was with Church seminaries, which he reported were established in "most of the high schools in Utah and those in Idaho, Colorado and Arizona with sufficient L.D.S. students attending." In response to the request, however, Brimhall presented an extensive essay titled "The Place of Seminaries and a Church University in Modern Education." In it he revisited some of the issues in BYU's so-called evolution crisis that had come to a head fifteen years earlier and argued that the Church's educational system should not drive a wedge between science and religion. He said,

> Perhaps no household has ever been more zealous for the faith of its children than the Latter-day Saint household. Nor has there anywhere been greater anxiety for scientific and research training. But there has grown up the feeling that these two branches of thought are incompatible.... That we can't have both. Some people have answered this problem by drawing into their shells. Preferring the faith of their fathers at any cost, yet unconsciously admitting a doubt as to its strength, they have

turned a deaf ear to science and to everything new or challenging. They have enclosed their faith, made a hot-house plant of it, and instead of strengthening it they have weakened it.... Their strength is not within their faith but in the ramparts they have built around it....

... There is no surer way to display our perfect faith in God than to welcome every truth that is disclosed by scientific research. We thus show that whatever else comes to light we abide in a perfect assurance of the triumph of God and his purposes.

He accepted the economic justification "for the closing of the few high schools and junior colleges which the church maintained" but lamented that "[LDS seminaries] appear to be no more than tacked on to the institutions with which they work, because a greater correlation between the scientific and religious thought could be achieved if the religious education could become an integral part of the school curriculum." He concluded that BYU was critically important to the Church's educational system, claiming, "The B.Y.U. [is] where all the work is designed to bring the seminary studies, the secular education and the more advanced studies of religion into a focus on the realities and needs of life."

Brimhall ended the essay by stating, "The Church recognizes the crying need of the age as that of coordinating the efforts of science and religion, of preparing men with hearts attuned to God and minds prepared to take advantage of the wonderful opportunities presented by our civilization." He said this was the unique mission of BYU.[18]

The Falling of a Mighty Oak

On December 9, 1931, Elder George Albert Smith visited Brimhall on his seventy-ninth birthday and saw how "sickness had broken him down."[19] By 1932, early rising was no longer a part of Brimhall's day, and "alternate hours were spent in his black, leather chair and his bed." His poor health—a constant concern throughout his life—became complicated as "a virulent influenza attacked him," and he became bedridden. On April 1, he wrote, "I am working with great desire—consuming much energy. The doctor just finished his daily visit. He thinks we are gaining, he and I." However, this conclusion proved false, and "from this point on there were no gains—in fact, he slowly lost ground."[20] Brimhall was suffering from several ailments, including kidney failure and an incapacitating rheumatism, which confined him to bed. Some believed that he also suffered from an untreatable cancer.[21] Doctors gave no hope of recovery. They could only prescribe pain medication, which in the end may have compounded and aggravated the effect the physical infirmities had on his mental condition.[22]

His granddaughter-in-law Esther Holbrook regularly attended him and observed,

> The world about him moved busily on. There were days, after his immediate needs were cared for, that he was left alone for hours at a time. He was heard to remark, "I get some enjoyment out of enduring without complaint...."

Professor Alice Louise Reynolds brightened those days, as she sat

Alice Louise Reynolds. Courtesy L. Tom Perry Special Collections.

at his bedside reading to him from his favorite literary selections.[23]

Amidst thoughts of the inevitable outcome, Brimhall did not seem to fear death but said that he and everyone feared "the law of decline ... the days of lingering, waiting, waiting, enduring the hammer strokes of time."[24] He was eventually killed by a discharge from a rifle, apparently by his own hand, in his home in Provo on July 29, 1932, four months short of his eightieth birthday. The *Provo Herald* announced the death in its Sunday headlines.

> The entire community and state were plunged into grief today at the word of the passing of Dr. George H. Brimhall, president-emeritus of the Brigham Young university, and active church and civic worker.
>
> Brimhall died late Friday afternoon at the family residence, 143 North Third East street. His dead body was first found at 5 o'clock by his wife, Mrs. Flora R. Brimhall, when she returned from a short shopping trip....
>
> Death was evidently caused by a bullet from a rifle which had been left in the basement of the home. The circumstances surrounding the tragedy are not known, since he was alone at the time, but it is thought that the gun discharged, perhaps accidentally, while he was examining it. He was known as a great lover of the out-of-doors, frequently went hunting and fishing, and prized his hunting weapons highly.[25]

Actually, it is likely that another person was at home at the time, the Brimhall's youngest son, Areo, who was twenty-two years old but mentally disabled because, according to

George H. Brimhall, ca. 1920. Courtesy L. Tom Perry Special Collections.

his mother, at the age of three he had "a fall of sixteen feet from a roof."[26]

The *Provo Herald* article went on to report that "members of his family observed that [Brimhall] had grown discouraged and that his restless spirit chafed under the long siege which had sapped his strength."[27] While many Utah newspapers simply reported that he died after a long illness,[28] his death certificate listed a "gunshot wound of head—self inflicted" as the primary cause of death.[29]

A general air of melancholy surrounded Brimhall's death as speculation about the way he left mortality spread. The day after his death, Elder James E. Talmage wrote in his journal,

> Word is published today of the death of our beloved brother, George H. Brimhall.... There is an element of tragedy in his passing. For many months he has been ill and his death has been expected; but, worn out in body and under a mental collapse, he seems to have been unable to await the next call of the messenger of death, and summoned him with the aid of a hunting rifle. I am sure the man was wholly irresponsible and that every circumstance will be taken into account in the final judgment as to his splendid life and sudden death.[30]

Word of Brimhall's death made its way overseas. John A. Widtsoe, who was serving as president of the Church's European mission, wrote to BYU President Franklin S. Harris:

> As I was traveling over the continent I picked up a News announcing the death of Brother Brimhall. I grieved, of course, to think that I should not again in this life meet this valiant defender of truth. He was always an inspiration to me. But, I was even more grieved when I reached Rotterdam to have questions put to me as to the manner of Brother Brimhall's death. Since that time statements about Brother Brimhall's death have come to me from at least a half dozen elders who have received information in private letters. I am quite unable to make any answer, and I have tried to be as guarded as possible in what I have said. Is there anything I should know to assist in turning the gossip that

seems to be spreading among the missionaries of these missions?[31]

In response, Harris wrote the following detailed explanation to Widtsoe:

Certainly this was a very tragic affair but I think no one who knows all the circumstances blames President Brimhall for the occurrence any more than if he had fallen from a house [horse?] or if he had been overcome by any other disaster for which he was in no way responsible.

He had been in bed for five and one half months with rheumatism and general poisoning of the system ... from which they seemed entirely unable to rid him. For months he seemed to preserve his balance completely but in time his nervous system was gradually undermined so that ... he was not at all himself and could not be held responsible for his actions no matter what they might have been.

It had not been thought that he needed anyone to watch him particularly however, and on the day of his death, his wife went out on an errand and while she was away he took a gun out of a closet in the room and then the fatal thing happened. It was very surprising because he had not been really able to stand by himself.... Of course the manner of his passing added to the gloom but it certainly did not lessen the respect of anyone intimately connected with the circumstances....

The unfortunate part of it is the fact that people outside and those who are not acquainted with the circumstances will not understand as those of us who are here do.[32]

Nearly two thousand people attended the funeral in the Provo Tabernacle on August 1, 1932.[33] During the services, President Harris eulogized his predecessor: "The passing of this great man is like the falling of a mighty oak that has been blown over by the accidental gust of a storm."[34]

Elder George Albert Smith, the senior ecclesiastical authority at the funeral, promised,

> He has gone home. Not to some obscure, undesirable place. He has been working for a place in the Celestial Kingdom. He has been seeking to have his name recorded in the Lamb's Book of Life. And I believe that if any man has accomplished that desirable thing, George H. Brimhall has accomplished it.

Calling him "a senior statesman," Smith said, "[Brimhall's service] filled a peculiar niche in our commonwealth and he will be missed by many of those who have appealed to him for advice and counsel," adding, "He was always found on the side of wisdom."[35] Longtime family friend A. O. Smoot, grandson of one of BYU's founders, noted that when his own family had "been bowed down in trouble and grief," they turned to Brimhall for "solace and comfort." Smoot further remarked that Brimhall "was able to give this solace in a most remarkable and inspiring way."[36]

In the end, Brimhall's death capped a life of unrelenting service to and interest in the Church, the university, and the students he mentored. But because of the way he died, it is tempting to conclude that although confident and successful on the surface, he may have possessed an underlying private pathos. Certainly the multifaceted nature of Brimhall's character—the inner struggles, the outer struggles, and the mental and physical anguish that he alone comprehended, especially at the end of his life— should make a person pause before claiming to understand him. But to conclude, as some have, that he intentionally took his life to cut short his incapacitation and pain[37] does not make sense either. Brimhall was a man who, for his whole life, thrived on enduring hardship, who saw suicide as "self-murder,"[38] and who was always meek and obedient to gospel principles.

The most likely explanation is the one expressed by Elder Talmage and President Harris, which states that "under a mental collapse,"[39] "he was not at all himself and could not be held responsible for his actions no matter what they might have been."[40] The Church's leadership and the community who knew Brimhall well maintained the highest respect for him.

In many ways, Brimhall's death in 1932 coincided with the end of a larger era and the beginning of another in the history of the Church, of Utah, of the United States, and of the world. Curtains closed while others opened on scenes everywhere. In the Church, influential writers and thinkers James E. Talmage and B. H. Roberts both died the next year, and that year the young J. Reuben Clark, under secretary of the U.S. Department of State and ambassador to Mexico, was called as a member of the First Presidency. The Great Depression hit rock bottom in 1932, and in response U.S. President Franklin D. Roosevelt was elected in November, commencing the dramatic changes of the New Deal. Prohibition was repealed in 1933, Utah being the deciding state that sealed its revocation. On world stage, Adolf Hitler came to power in 1933, and international conflicts began a course of inevitable collision that soon erupted into World War II. Two years later, in 1935, the Mechanic Arts Building, which stood next to the Maeser Memorial on BYU's upper campus, the second building to be constructed there, was greatly expanded and refurbished and renamed the George H. Brimhall Building, as a lasting tribute to his memory.[41]

Notes

Epigraph quoted from "Reflection" in *Long and Short Range Arrows,* comp. and ed. Harrison R. Merrill and Alice L. Reynolds, 2d ed. (Provo, Utah: Brigham Young University Press, 1936), 195. It was apparently written in 1928 and read by Jennie Brimhall Knight at the dedication of the George H. Brimhall Building in October 1935.

1. Jennie H. Groberg and Delbert V. Groberg, *Biography Collection: George H. Brimhall* (n.p.: Alsina Elizabeth Brimhall Holbrook Family, 1988), 215A; *Tributes to George H. Brimhall* (n.p.: Alsina Elizabeth Brimhall Holbrook Family, [1988]), 16–18; J. Marinus Jensen, *History of Brigham Young University* (n.p.: n.p., 1942), 63; Groberg and Groberg, *Biography Collection,* 229. In recognition of his contributions, Brimhall was awarded an Honorary Doctorate of Laws on June 27, 1921. Alice L. Reynolds, "Dr. George H. Brimhall," *Young Woman's Journal* 32, no. 7 (July 1921): 383.

2. David J. Whittaker, "George H. Brimhall," in Groberg and Groberg, *Biography Collection,* 244.

3. Raymond Brimhall Holbrook and Esther Hamilton Holbrook, *The Tall Pine Tree: The Life and Work of George H. Brimhall* (n.p.: By the authors, 1988), 171.

4. Holbrook and Holbrook, *Tall Pine Tree,* 92; see also Brimhall, *Long and Short Range Arrows,* 16.

5. George H. Brimhall to Franklin S. Harris, January 4, 1924, Franklin S. Harris Presidential Papers, L. Tom Perry Special Collections, Harold B. Lee Library, Brigham Young University, Provo, Utah. This sentiment may not have been shared by all his family. According to Newell G. Bringhurst, Brimhall's daughter Fawn McKay was "embittered toward BYU because of its treatment of her father." Newell G. Bringhurst, *Fawn McKay Brodie: A Biographer's Life* (Norman: University of Oklahoma Press, 1999), 46.

6. Brimhall, *Long and Short Range Arrows,* 7.

7. Ernest L. Wilkinson, ed., *Brigham Young University: The First One Hundred Years,* 4 vols. (Provo, Utah: Brigham Young University Press, 1975), 1:520.

8. "Address by President Heber J. Grant," October 16, 1935, in *Tributes,* 28; Alice J. Louise Reynolds, "Excerpts from Biographical Sketch of George H. Brimhall, in *Tributes,* 143; George H. Brimhall to Elsie Hogan, November 30, 1931, in George H. Brimhall, *MIA Lessons for the Advanced Senior Class* (n.p.: Alsina Elizabeth Brimhall Holbrook Family, [1988]), 380; see Heber J. Grant to George H. Brimhall, April 22, 1917, George H. Brimhall Presidential Papers, Perry Special Collections; and Holbrook and Holbrook, *Tall Pine Tree,* 97–98.

9. Clarissa A. Beesley to George H. Brimhall, March 5, 1931, in *Tributes,* 69.

10. Amy Brown Lyman, ed., "Relief Society Lessons by George H. Brimhall," 322, Brimhall Presidential Papers.

11. Amy Brown Lyman to George H. Brimhall, March 30, 1923, Brimhall Presidential Papers.

12. George H. Brimhall to Susa Young Gates, October 6, 1904, Brimhall Presidential Papers.

13. Flora Robertson Brimhall, Life Sketch, in Groberg and Groberg, *Biography Collection,* 306.

14. George H. Brimhall, *Diary of George H. Brimhall,* 2 vols. (n.p.: Alsina Elizabeth Brimhall Holbrook Family, [1990]), 2:868, January 7 and 14, 1922.

15. Heber J. Grant to George H. Brimhall, September 21, 1921, in *Tributes,* 19.

16. Wilkinson, *First One Hundred Years,* 2:68–77.

17. Adam S. Bennion to George H. Brimhall, March 4, 1926, in George H. Brimhall, *Longer Talks* (n.p.: Alsina Elizabeth Brimhall Holbrook Family, [1988]), 147.

18. "The Place of Seminaries and a Church University in Modern Education," in Brimhall, *Longer Talks,* 134–35, 146, 147.

19. George Albert Smith, funeral address, in *Tributes,* 395.

20. Holbrook and Holbrook, *Tall Pine Tree,* 180.

21. Interview with John H. Groberg, March 20, 2006. The kidney failure, or renal failure, is listed as "Uremic Poisoning" on Brimhall's death certificate as a contributing cause of death.

22. Holbrook and Holbrook, *Tall Pine Tree,* 180. The medical prescriptions for pain at that time may have included limited amounts of alcohol, which, if prescribed, could reduce a patient's inhibitions.

23. Holbrook and Holbrook, *Tall Pine Tree,* 180. In the appendix to his book, *Solemn Covenant: The Mormon Polygamous Passage* (Urbana: University of Illinois Press, 1992), [397], B. Carmon Hardy lists Alice Reynolds as a third wife to George H. Brimhall, citing a 1943 letter from Fawn Brodie, Brimhall's granddaughter, to Claire Noall, and an interview conducted by Newell Bringhurst, biographer of Fawn Brodie. No marriage date is given. In the letter, Brodie writes, "You see, only last summer I learned for the first time that my own grandfather had three wives instead of two, as everyone believed. My mother [Brimhall's daughter] never knew it—although the third wife was my grandfather's secretary and very ubiquitous indeed" (Fawn Brodie to Claire Noall, December 31, 1943, Matthew Frederick and Claire Wilcox Noall Papers, University of Utah Marriott Library, Manuscripts Division, Salt Lake City). The letter does not give the name of the supposed third wife. Reynolds's name was introduced in Bringhurst's interview with Fawn Brodie's sister Flora Crawford. Bringhurst asked Crawford, "How did you get a sense that they were married?" Crawford answered, "I don't know. I just got a sense of it, because we knew who Mother's [Brimhall's daughter] half-sisters and brothers were—that he'd been married to two women that were alive. Arial—who was two years old then [*sic*] I—Areial and I were very close, and he used to tell me that.... So I haven't any proof" (Flora Crawford, oral history interview, September 26, 1988, 62, Newell Bringhurst Collection, University of Utah Marriott Library, Salt Lake City). The half brothers and sisters referred to by Crawford were undoubtedly the children of Brimhall's first wife, Alsina Wilkins. "Ariel" or "Areial" was probably Brimhall's and Flora's youngest child, Areo, who was mentally incapacitated. Bringhurst's investigation of this matter is found in Bringhurst, *Fawn McKay Brodie,* 273n20, in which he states that another sister of Fawn Brodie, Barbara Smith, claimed that "according to family tradition, her grandfather traveled to

southern California with Alice Louise Reynolds in the early twentieth century, purportedly to attend an educator's convention but primarily to cross the border to Mexico secretly so that they could be married."

Brimhall's diaries chronicle a trip to Los Angeles (Brimhall, *Diary*, 1:478–58, July 6–July 16, 1907) to attend the National Educational Association (NEA) convention. Alice Reynolds's biographer confirms Reynolds's attendance at the same convention (Amy Brown Lyman, *A Lighter of Lamps: The Life Story of Alice Louise Reynolds* [Provo, Utah: Alice Louise Reynolds Club, 1947], 29). Brimhall records in his diary that prior to leaving Salt Lake City by train he called on George Reynolds, Alice Reynolds's father (Brimhall, *Diary*, 1:478, July 6, 1907). Brimhall roomed with Superintendent Cummings, but also visited and stayed at least one night with others, but always in the Los Angeles area. The convention lasted from Monday, July 8, to Friday, July 12, 1907. According to Brimhall's diaries, he attended the convention for at least part of each of those days. At the conclusion of the convention, he traveled with a Brother Mumford to San Francisco, and Brimhall left San Francisco for Utah on Sunday, July 14, 1907, arriving in Salt Lake City on July 16 (Brimhall, *Diary*, 1:480–86, July 8–16, 1907). Except for the diary entry of July 6, 1907, listing Alice Reynolds as one of those traveling to the Los Angeles convention, no other mention is made of her during this trip.

Alice Louise Reynolds became a member of the BYA faculty in 1894. She was the daughter of George Reynolds, one of the First Seven Presidents of the Seventy and secretary to the First Presidency of the Church (Lyman, *Lighter of Lamps*, 2–3, 27). Apparently, her sister, Florence Reynolds, married Benjamin Cluff Jr., Brimhall's predecessor at BYU, as a post-Manifesto plural wife in 1900 or possibly earlier. See Julie Hemming Savage, "Hannah Grover Hegsted and Post-Manifesto Plural Marriage," *Dialogue: A Journal of Mormon Thought* 26, no. 3 (Fall 1993): 112. For general information, see Wilkinson, *First One Hundred Years*, 1:377, 378; "Alice L. Reynolds and Brigham Young University," *BYU History, L. Tom Perry Special Collections*, http://lib.byu.edu/sites/byuhistory/

universityhistory/pst/alicereynolds/ (accessed May 10, 2010); and Alice Louise Reynolds, Autobiography, typescript, Perry Special Collections. The authors found nothing in Brimhall's records or memorabilia, nor in Reynolds's, to suggest that Brimhall was ever married to Alice Louise Reynolds.

24. A. O. Smoot, funeral address, in *Tributes,* 379. Smoot quoted Brimhall's own words given at a funeral of a boyhood friend.

25. "Dr. George H. Brimhall Meets Death at Home," *Provo Herald,* July 31, 1932, 1.

26. Brimhall, Life Sketch, in Groberg and Groberg, *Biography Collection,* 306.

27. "Dr. George H. Brimhall Meets Death at Home," 1.

28. See, for example, "President Emeritus of Brigham Young University Dies," *Deseret News,* July 30, 1932, 1.

29. George H. Brimhall Certificate of Death, in possession of Joseph H. Groberg, Idaho Falls, Idaho. No autopsy or criminal investigation was conducted; and though there has never been any evidence that he died in any way other than a self-inflicted wound, what appears to be a question mark appears to be penciled in next to the cause-of-death section on the certificate. Who wrote it and how late it was written is unknown.

30. James E. Talmage, Diary, typescript, 19–20, July 30, 1932, James E. Talmage Papers, Perry Special Collections.

31. John A. Widtsoe to Franklin S. Harris, September 7, 1932, Harris Presidential Papers.

32. Franklin S. Harris to John A. Widtsoe, September 21, 1932, Harris Presidential Papers.

33. "Tributes Paid to Brimhall," *Provo Herald,* August 2, 1932, 1.

34. Franklin S. Harris, funeral address, in *Tributes,* 387.

35. George Albert Smith, funeral address, in *Tributes,* 392, 393, 394–95.

36. A. O. Smoot, funeral address, in *Tributes,* 378.

37. Gary James Bergera and Ronald Priddis, *Brigham Young University: A House of Faith* (Salt Lake City: Signature Books, 1985), 13.

38. "Scholarship an Implement to Manhood," January 12, 1909, in George H. Brimhall, *BYU Devotional Talks,* 2 vols. (n.p.: Alsina Elizabeth Brimhall Holbrook Family, 1988), 1:215.

39. Talmage, Diary, 20, July 30, 1932.

40. Harris to Widtsoe, September 21, 1932.

41. The building was extensively remodeled in 1988 and in 2005. After the last remodeling it was rededicated by Brimhall's great-grandson Elder John H. Groberg at the request of the Church Board of Education. See chapter 5 note 119.

Appendix A

George H. Brimhall's Family

In June 1907, George Brimhall traveled with his daughter Jennie and members of the Knight family to see if they could locate the graves of members of both families who had died in winter 1846–47, during the Mormon exodus from Nauvoo, and who were buried on the Ponca Indian reservation about 120 miles northwest of Omaha, Nebraska. Then they traveled to Galesburg, Illinois, to see if Brimhall could locate his half-brother, the son of his father's first wife, Lucretia, who had stayed behind in Nauvoo. George wrote in his journal for that month:

> Jennie B. and I took East Galesburg car to Farenham St., then walked south to 318 South. There on the south-east corner of the block we found a frame house with east and south fronts, barn in rear. A horse stood harnessed near the barn—a buggy stood just north of the house and a light wagon just back of the barn. Chickens in an enclosure fed in the back

yard; two jersey cows stood just north of the barn. The whole place bore an air of cleanliness and thrift.

We entered the east gate, walked along the planks to the porch, stepped up and knocked. After I had opened the wire door a young lady came to the door and said, "Won't you come in?" I said, "Well my name is Brimhall." "Oh, one of pap's cousins I presume." "I am his brother." With a look of utter surprise she said "Sit down and I will call papa." She went out. After a pause of perhaps two minutes, in came a man who said, "You claim to be a Brimhall." "I am one," said I. "Bring a lamp", he said as the twilight had gathered. The young woman brot a little lamp, placed it on the piano and the man surveyed me and said, "So you are a Brimhall." "Yes, I am son of George W. Brimhall." "Well," he said, "You don't look much like the picture I saw."

We shook hands. He bade me welcome and I introduced my daughter. . . . The man was my brother Rufus Brimhall, 61 yrs of age whom I had never seen before. He is bowed with overwork and pale from illness. . . .

. . . We talked of father, <u>my</u> father at first then <u>our</u> father.[1]

Later that same summer, while visiting in Canada, George received a telegram that his younger brother Emer had been killed by lightning in Utah. George said his greatest thrill in life had been giving half his crop to Emer and wrote: "We have always been friends as well as brothers." For the days immediately after Emer's death, George's journal reads:

Thurs. 29. Up at 4 from our bed in Wash's cabin. Off for home at 5. . . .

Fri. 30. Up at 3. Train at 4 have been in terrible grief all way homeward.

Sat. 31. Salt Lake 8: 30 am. Provo 6:30 pm. Sad, sad, sad. Spanish Fork 9:30, Buggy.

Sun. Sept. 1. Today we laid Emer in the grave. One of the darkest days of my life. My heart is heavy and at times seems ready to burst with sorrow.[2]

Throughout his life as a teacher and as an administrator, including the time he served as president of Brigham Young University, George had many other responsibilities and interests. On behalf of the Church Board of Education, he traveled by train and buggy to strengthen religious education all over Utah and in Idaho, California, Arizona, Colorado, Wyoming, Canada, and Mexico. He worked hard on MIA manuals and traveled around the Church to encourage and train MIA workers. He held callings in his ward and stake and faithfully attended a Sunday morning prayer circle when he was in Provo. He was often assigned to speak in stake conferences and to participate in general conferences. George also worked with mission presidents to train missionaries.

Personally, he farmed and ranched in Spanish Fork Canyon and in Canada and Provo. He shod horses, milked cows, built fences, and did other chores. George sought every opportunity to be outdoors, riding horses, camping, fishing, hunting, and sightseeing. He was active in civic affairs, pushing for national prohibition, lobbying the state legislature for recognition of teachers, and even fighting to prevent the railroad from moving its station from Academy Avenue in Provo. He served as an officer of the Republican Party and dabbled in mining stock, usually in association with Jessie Knight, and also in real estate. But more than any other thing, George valued his time to be with and serve his family.[3]

Brimhall Gallery opening family photograph, April 4, 1988

Row 1 (sitting on floor, left to right)
Tyler Ownes
Joseph S. Tingey
Clarissa Kay Stebbing
William Luke Stebbing
Bradley Brown
Emily Brown
Whitney Owens
Jordan Mitchell
Emily Mitchell
Damion Mitchell
Deja Mitchell
Andrew Groberg
Clair Osborn
Ruthie Holbrook
John Lafayette Holbrook
Pamela Groberg
Kaila Corinne Fox
Rachel Groberg
Heidi Groberg
Rebecca Groberg

Row 2 (left to right)
Iona Brimhall Stevens
Richard W. Brown
Dana L. Brown
Susan Eliason
Sandra Pehrson
Marva Stevens Allen
Bradley R. Carlson
Barbara J. Carlson

Sylvia Caldwell
Nora Mae B. Brown
Raymon H. Brown
Laura Alsina Groberg
Brenda Marie Groberg
Gretchen Groberg
Anna Marie Groberg
Jeanne Pratt Groberg
Joseph H. Groberg
Samuel Lewis Groberg
Rosalee Fritzen
Sarah Marie Groberg
Carolyn Blair
Anny Fritzen
Marilyn Groberg Powell
Samuel P. Powell (baby)
James G. Powell
J. Matthew Powell
Thomas O. Powell (on lap)
Mike Groberg
John Cummings
Dahlena Cummings
Stephen C. Tingey
Benjamin Tingey (on lap)
Nancy Jean Groberg Tingey

Row 3 (left to right)
Beverly Brimhall Bowen
Rebecca Brown Sauerland
Elizabeth Brown
Rusty Brown

Jennifer K. Brown
Sandra S. Brown
Albert H. Brown
Mark Haymore
Jess Birtcher
Stanley E. Stebbing
Sam Edwin Stebbing (on lap)
JoAnn Braithwaite Stebbing
Bonnie J. Groberg
Annie Groberg (on lap)
George H. Groberg
Susan Braithwaite
Jane Anderson Braithwaite
Lafayette Robert Anderson
Madge Greaves Anderson
Lynette Anderson Christensen
Todd Groberg
John Holbrook Groberg
Jean Sabin Groberg
Mary Jane Fritzen
Kevin Del Lambert
Jenette Blair Lambert
Mary Holbrook
Matthew M. Holbrook
Judith M. Holbrook
Beth Groberg Stratton

Row 4 (left to right)
Noram B. Lewis
Rulon W. Brimhall
Francis Ray Brown
Nancy Dahlquist
Helen Holbrook Dahlquist
Elaine Holbrook Haymore
Elizabeth Holbrook Berry
Vera Holbrook Heninger
Maurice King Heninger
Oliver R. Smith
Golden H. Brimhall
Barbara McKay Smith
Janelle Brimhall Lysenko
James G. Blair
W. Smoot Brimhall
Maurine Jones Brimhall
Lisa Sabey
David Sabey (in arms)
Margaret Blair Young
Julia Groberg Blair
Jennie Holbrook Groberg
Delbert V. Groberg
Joye Cummings
Joseph L. Cummings

Row 5 (left to right)
Bonnie Brimhall Kofford
Roselyn Burton Brimhall
James Wesley Brimhall
Kimberly Crapo

Mary Lee Dahlquist Sessions
Timothy Elliott Sessions
Kristen Crapo
Cynthia Berry
Michelle Berry
Nancy Spendlove Moench
Jennifer Moench
Camille Calder Spendlove
David C. Spendlove
Lisa Calder Spendlove
Joan Osborn
Karl Owens
Elizabeth Groberg Owens
Troy J. Garner
Jane Groberg Garner
Gloria Groberg Hubble
Richard H. Groberg
Mark Sabey
Brian Sabey (in arms)
Delbert Wallace Blair
Kathleen Naumann Blair
Lois Cummings
Erma J. Severson
Suzanne McKay
Kathryn Bell
Diane Filimachala
Jane Axson

Row 6 (left to right)
Lyman Brimhall Stevens
LeGrande Allen

Earl B. Telford
Bernice Telford
Marjorie Bown Whatcott
Calvin D. Whatcott
Kevin Bown Whatcott
Carolee Whatcott
David Kay Berry
Sharon Berry
Louine Hunter
David J. Hunter
Carol Crandall Spendlove
J. Clifton Spendlove
Janice Spendlove Moreland
Vincent S. Moreland
Lewis Groberg
David H. Groberg
Lorraine Groberg
Robert G. Blair
Jonathan Pratt Groberg
Ben Blair
Kristin B. Osborn
Dean Osborn
Frances Brimhall Osborn
George L. Cummings
Marilyn McKay
Thomas B. McKay
Julian William (Bill) Cummings
Ronald McKay Smith

George's family included his two wives, his parents, and his wives' parents and their brothers and sisters. It included his nine siblings and their families and his two half-brothers and half-sister by his father's first wife. But most importantly, it included his thirteen children who grew to maturity and their spouses and children along with his grandchildren. George felt an attachment to and responsibility for each one.

Notes

1. George H. Brimhall, *Diary of George H. Brimhall,* 2 vols. (n.p.: Alsina Elizabeth Brimhall Holbrook Family, [1990]), 1:465–66, June 1907.

2. Brimhall, *Diary,* 2:1058, 1927–28; 1:445–45, August 28–September 1, 1907.

3. See, for example, Brimhall, *Diary,* 1:542, July 26, 1909.

The family names and dates in this appendix were compiled for the authors by Mary Jane Fritzen in 2008 with the best information available to her at that time. The authors acknowledge that there may be errors and omissions in this information.

George Henry Brimhall (b. 1852; d. 1932)
married
(1) Alsina Elizabeth Wilkins (b. 1856; m. 1874; d. 1926)

1. Lucy Jane (b. 1875; d. 1957)
2. Alsina Elisabeth (b. 1876; d. 1960)
3. George Washington (b. 1878; d. 1954)
4. Mark Henry (b. 1880; d. 1965)
5. Wells Lovett (b. 1882; d. 1947)
6. Milton Albert (b. 1883; d. 1884)

(2) Flora McDonald Robertson (b. 1865; m. 1885; d. 1950)

1. Dean Robertson (b. 1886; d. 1972)
2. Fay Robertson (b. 1889 [twin]; d. 1972)
3. Fawn Robertson (b. 1889 [twin]; d. 1960)
4. Burns Robertson (b. 1892; d. 1976)
5. Ruth Afton (b. 1895; d. 1969)
6. Paul Robertson (b. 1898; d. 1977)
7. Alta (b. 1901; d. 1903)
8. Golden Henry (b. 1906; d. 2000)
9. Areo Robertson (b. 1909; d. 1980)

Lucy Jane Brimhall (b. 1875; d. 1957)
married
Jesse William Knight (b. 1874; m. 1899; d. 1956)

1. Richard Knight (b. 1911; d. 1995)
    married
    Julia Alta Gale Stewart (m. 1935 (div))

2. Philip Staker Maycock Knight (b. 1915; d. 1993)
married
Ellen Binns (m. 1937)

Alsina Elisabeth Brimhall (b. 1876; d. 1960)
married
Lafayette Hinckley Holbrook (b. 1877; m. 1901; d. 1969)

1. Raymond Brimhall Holbrook (b. 1902; d. 1989)
married
Esther Ruth Hamilton (m. 1928)
2. Rachel Holbrook (b. 1903; d. 1946)
married
Robert Clair Anderson (m. 1927)
3. George Blaine Holbrook (b. 1906; d. 1924)
4. Jennie Holbrook (b. 1908; d. 2004)
married
Delbert Valentine Groberg (m. 1930)
5. Mary Holbrook (b. 1910; d. 1977)
married
Benjamin Alva Maxwell (m. 1932)
6. Ruth Holbrook (b. 1912; d. 1983)
married
Francis Ray Brown (m. 1932)
7. Elizabeth Holbrook (b. 1914; d. 2000)
married
Alonzo Kay Berry (m. 1934)
8. Jean Holbrook (b. 1915; d. 1923)
9. Helen Holbrook (b. 1917)
married
Carlyle "A" Dahlquist (m. 1941)
10. Vera Holbrook (b. 1918; d. 2005)
married
Maurice King Heninger (m. 1941)

11. Alsina Elaine Holbrook (b. 1920)

    married

    John Arnold Haymore (m. 1938 (div))

George Washington Brimhall (b. 1878; d. 1954)
married
Harriet Woolf (b. 1883; m. 1902; d. 1967)

1. Gladys Brimhall (b. 1902; d. 1974)

   married

   Pearson Harris Corbett (m. 1926)

2. George Martin Brimhall (b. 1904; d. 1960)

   married

   Ethel June Huntsman

3. Helen Brimhall (b. 1908; d. 1992)

   married

   Byron James Brown

4. Alma Devoe Brimhall (b. 1912; d. 2000)

   married

   Beth Peters (m. 1939)

5. Barbara Claire Brimhall (b. 1922; d. 2007)

   married

   Mark Stewart Howe

6. (Stillborn) Brimhall (b. 1924; d. 1924)

Mark Henry Brimhall (b. 1880; d. 1965)
married
(1) Guinevere Ricks Smellie (b. 1886; m. 1905; d. 1943)

1. Iona Smellie Brimhall (b. 1905; d. 2000)

   married

   Kenneth Richards Stevens (m. 1926)

2. Jennie Winona Brimhall (b. 1907; d. 1976)

   married

   (1) Newell Wayne Bown (m. 1931)

   (2) David Lorenzo Cox (m. 1967)

3. Beth Smellie Brimhall (b. 1910; d. 1910)
4. Erma Brimhall (b. 1914; d. 1914)
5. Mark Bruce Brimhall (b. 1916; d. 1916)
6. Bessie Brimhall (b. 1917; d. 1917)
7. Eloise Brimhall (b. 1922; d. 1922)

(2) Martha Alice Garfield (b. 1887; m. 1944; d. 1949)

Wells Lovett Brimhall (b. 1882; d. 1947)
married
Fern Smoot (b. 1885; m. 1908; d. 1974)

1. Sina Brimhall (b. 1910; d. 1973)
   married
   Gordon McKay Stevenson (m. 1932)
2. Wells Smoot Brimhall (b. 1914)
   married
   (1) Viva Maurine Jones (m. 1935)
   (2) Helena Call Jacobsen (m. 2002)
3. Victor Owen Brimhall (b. 1920)
   married
   Anabelle McQuown (m. 1948)

Dean Robertson Brimhall (b. 1886; d. 1972)
married
Lila Eccles (b. 1891; m. 1917; d. 1980)

1. McKean Eccles Brimhall (b. 1918; d. 1944)
   married
   Ruth Bernice Carlquist
2. James Eccles Brimhall (b. 1920; d. 1920)
3. Frances Brimhall (b. 1923)
   married
   Hal W. Osborn

Fay Robertson Brimhall (b. 1889; d. 1972)
married
Julian Moses Cummings (b. 1884; m. 1909; d. 1963)

1. Mary Fay Cummings (b. 1910; d. 1974)
    married
    (1) Henry Wilford Struhs (m. 1929 (div))
    (2) Norman Leroy Stiles (m. 1943)
2. (Stillborn) Cummings (b. 1912)
3. Ruth Cummings (b. 1913; d. 1969)
    married
    August Henry Carl Niebuhr (m. 1932 (div))
4. Julian William Cummings (b. 1915; d. 2002)
    married
    (1) Marjorie Louise Caine (m. 1941 (div))
    (2) Kay Kemppel
5. John Earl Cummings (b. 1917; d. 1984)
    married
    Lucetta Walker (m. 1943)
6. George Lawrence Cummings (b. 1919; d. 2000)
    married
    (1) Vera Pauline Neal (m. 1941)
    (2) Lois Loika Heue (m. 1946)
7. Joseph Lorraine Cummings (b. 1922; d. 2004)
    married
    Joye Jensen (m. 1949)
8. Beth Cummings (b. 1924; d. 2003)
    married
    Alma Lyle Jensen (m. 1942)

**Fawn Robertson Brimhall (b. 1889; d. 1960)
married
Thomas Evans McKay (b. 1876; m. 1912; d. 1958)**

1. Flora Jeannette McKay (b. 1913; d. 2001)
    married
    (1) Oren Leslie Jensen (m. 1935)
    (2) Glen Donald Crawford (m. 1964 (div))
2. Fawn McKay (b. 1915; d. 1981)
    married
    Bernard Brodie (m. 1936)
3. Thomas Brimhall McKay (b. 1917; d. 2004)
    married
    (1) Sarah Knowlton (m. 1941)
    (2) Suzanne Wilson Bell (m. 1967)
4. Barbara Fay McKay (b. 1920; d. 2005)
    married
    Oliver Rollin Smith (m. 1942)
5. Marjorie Louise McKay (b. 1925)
    married
    Richard Young Card (m. 1942)

**Burns Robertson Brimhall (b. 1892; d. 1976)
married
(1) Alberta Mariah Grotegut (m. 1917 (div))**

1. Bernice Brimhall (b. 1918; d. 2006)
    married
    (1) Clayton Whitehead (m. 1937)
    (2) Franklin Bowen (m. 1951)
    (3) Earl Telford (m. 1971)
2. Caroline Brimhall
    married
    Lynn B. Hopkin

3. Flora Brimhall
   married
   (1) Robert Mastronardi (div)
   (2) Gary Stimpson

(2) Florence Palmer

Ruth Afton Brimhall (b. 1895; d. 1969)
married
Eugene Crandall (b. 1887; m. 1921; d. 1957)

1. Betty Ruth Crandall (b. 1921)
   married
   Ebb Pounds (m. 1948)
2. Carol Crandall (b. 1926)
   married
   J. Clifton Spendlove (m. 1944)
3. ValGene Crandall (b. 1930)
   married
   Karen Amanda Price (m. 1956)

Paul Robertson Brimhall (b. 1898; d. 1977)
married
Margaret Viola Heinback (m. 1931 (div); d. 1984)

1. William Dean Brimhall (b. 1929; d. 2005)
   married
   Mary Stathopulas
2. Martha Flora Brimhall (b. 1932)
   married
   Neil Anthony Daniele (b. 1930)
3. George Heinbach Brimhall (b. 1933)
   married
   Patty Thulin
4. James Bruce Brimhall (b. 1935; d. 1977)

5. John Lawrence Brimhall (b. 1937)
   married
   Phyllis Gibbs (m. 1966)

**Golden Henry Brimhall (b. 1906; d. 2000)
married
Bessie Lucilla Smith (m. 1935)**

1. Bryann Brimhall
   married
   Cole
2. Lucinda Brimhall
   married
   Mills

Appendix B

George H. Brimhall's Sermonettes

"Students remembered George H. Brimhall for his four-minute inspirational talks. On one occasion Brimhall told his audience that too much hurry causes people to lose moments that should have been savored. Calling on his recent experience of driving through Orem's flowering peach orchards, he concluded, 'When you drive through heaven, stop and look.'"[1]

In 1934, shortly after Brimhall's death, BYU Press published *Long and Short Range Arrows,* a small book containing some of his short talks or sermonettes to the student body, some of his poetry, and a biographical sketch by Alice Louise Reynolds. In the book's introduction, Franklin S. Harris wrote: "[Brimhall] was the embodiment of loyalty—loyalty to his church, to the institution he served so long, to his friends, and to every worthy cause.... We are glad that in these sermonettes we shall find it possible again to sit under his tuition."[2]

The following sermonettes are illustrative of these short talks Brimhall gave to the BYU student body during his service as president emeritus. In many instances they are decidedly dated, but in every instance they contain the flavor of Brimhall's famous devotional speeches.

Notes

1. Ernest L. Wilkinson, ed., *Brigham Young University: The First One Hundred Years,* 4 vols. (Provo, Utah: Brigham Young University Press, 1975), 2:309.

2. George H. Brimhall, *Long and Short Range Arrows,* comp. and ed. Harrison R. Merrill and Alice L. Reynolds, 2d ed. (Provo, Utah: Brigham Young University Press, 1936), 6.

Long and Short Range Arrows

... A few evenings ago in Ogden canyon, an automobile headed from Huntsville towards Ogden was making good time. The highway was banked on both sides with snow, pushed high by the snow [plow], leaving room for passing, provided each vehicle kept close to its bank. On a curve the car came suddenly upon a bob-sled which was coming up the canyon in the middle of the track. The driver of the car had the alternative of striking the sled or plunging into the snow bank on the river side of the track. He chose the latter. The car kept its wheels but stuck fast in the snow. One of the occupants of the sled, looking back, saw the snow-bound condition of the auto, called to the [sled] driver to stop, and went to the aid of the chauffeur.

The driver of the car met the man from the sled with the declaration, "It was my fault, I was coming a little too fast; you people did not have time to give me passing room." The man from the bob-sled party shouted to his companions: "Come back! Here is a real gentleman!"

The occupants of the sled piled out and the car was soon on the road.

Every one of the bob-sleigh party thought, and some of them said in substance: "It is a rare thing to find a man who will not dodge behind some tree of self-justification when he gets into trouble, by not giving the other fellow a full chance."

This circumstance caused me to wish for more real gentlemen in all the highways of life, from the home circle to international council chambers. Just the confession, "It was my fault, I was going too fast," would be a signal for more home happiness and possibly a world-peace.

[George H. Brimhall, "Long and Short Range Arrows," in *Long and Short Range Arrows,* comp. and ed. Harrison R. Merrill and Alice L. Reynolds, 2d ed. (Provo, Utah: Brigham Young University Press, 1936), 19–20.]

Two Directions at the Same Time

I was driving a buggy up Spanish Fork canyon years ago. By my side sat my boy. A freight train came thundering along, and we speeded up the team for the purpose of enjoying the company of the great moving mass. The boy spoke up, saying, "Pa, look." And I said, "Look, what do you see?" "A fellow going two directions at the same time." And sure enough, there was a man on the top of the train, running to the rear. He was running west and the train was carrying him east.

The lad had heard me say that people could not go in two directions at the same time, and here was evidence against my assertion. I said, "Well, what is going to happen?" The youngster replied, "He will have to stop or be dumped off."

The train sped on but it left a lesson with us.

The warning has been given by our President: "Stop going in a direction opposite to that of our school, or you will be dumped off."

The direction of the institution is toward the rising sun, the direction of a better school, a bigger school; those who remain with it must be in the direction of the bigger, better students.

So it is with me and my country, the glorious government of the United States. It is moving toward greater liberty, more magnificent achievement, better laws. It is an institution noted for order and moral growth. It is on up-grade, going toward the sunrise. When my country moves in the direction of the amendment and repeal, I must not pursue the policy of seeking the nullification of laws by breaking them. *[The Eighteenth Amendment to the U.S. Constitution (the Prohibition Amendment) was passed January 29, 1919. It was repealed by the Twenty-first Amendment passed December 5, 1933.]* I cannot long move backward while my country moves forward or my jump-off is certain.

My Church is moving in the direction of glorifying God with its good work in the spread of truth, by the use of its resources, and by its valor in opposing iniquity.

If my life is counter to, instead of parallel with, that of my Church and my fellow men; if I am not honest with the Lord in my tithes and honest with my fellow men in letting their property alone and in paying my debts, the same inevitable fate awaits me as awaited the man on the train, unless he changed his course—I shall be dumped off.

Lives of double direction are short and disastrous.

[George H. Brimhall, "Two Directions at the Same Time," in *Long and Short Range Arrows,* comp. and ed. Harrison R. Merrill and Alice L. Reynolds, 2d ed. (Provo, Utah: Brigham Young University Press, 1936), 40–41.]

Joy of Earning

During the vacation I took a little ride of about three thousand miles by automobile and I saw a number of things that were new to me. Of the things that I saw and heard, the conquests of some of our boys gave me the greatest thrill.

I found one young man, married, conducting the largest amusement pavilion on the coast. He was one of our Utah Valley boys and in making inquiry about him I found he had a good position, and the man who has the money invested said, "And he has earned it. We give him four hundred dollars a month and he earns every cent of it. He has made the thing pay by hard work."

In getting tickets for a theater, one of the largest amusement places in Los Angeles, we ran up against another Utah Valley boy, one who has been here at school. He was in the office as manager of that great concern. He had got into that position partly through a recommendation from here, but he had earned that recommendation. I know something about where it came from, and he had earned it. He earned the place he occupies as manager of that institution.

Big thing, this earning process! ... I have also a few lines here which I will read to you:

"Better to leave to the children the ability to earn a dollar whenever they need it than to leave them a million to spend whenever they want. The joy of earning is greater than the joy of spending."

"Inherited wealth is too often the doom of genuine independence."

"It takes more than an ordinary offspring to carry an inherited estate. It was a wise man who said: 'I'll leave my children projects that will make them wealthy if they will be honest and work hard, or that will make them poor if they won't work.'"

"Wealth that comes from the power to earn belongs to the one who obtains."

"Wealth inherited is what the living has borrowed from the dead."

"The joy of earning is a high point in living. The gifts of the earner are completely his own."

And now may I conclude by saying as I have said before: The students who receive unearned credit have placed upon their shoulders a handicap.

I once had a conversation with a man who had found four thousand dollars in one of the forests of Arizona. I said: "What did you do with it?"

He said: "I hunted the owner until I found him. He gave me a hundred dollars."

"Were you sorry that you gave the money up?"

He said: "No."

I said: "Why?"

He said: "Dr. Brimhall, it would be a curse to me, from my point of view. I want what I earn."

So I repeat—that the joy of earning is next to the highest apex of enjoyment.

[George H. Brimhall, "Joy of Earning," in *Long and Short Range Arrows,* comp. and ed. Harrison R. Merrill and Alice L. Reynolds, 2d ed. (Provo, Utah: Brigham Young University Press, 1936), 94–96.]

The Church of My Choice

I can't hope that any of you will ever think a tenth as much about what I shall say as I have thought in preparing it. I was to present to you this morning the Church of my choice. I have selected the characteristics that are not common with other churches. Some of them may be found in other churches, but they are not common to other churches.

First: It is linked to Heaven by divine authority and it doesn't need to have its history traced through the ages to prove its origin.

Second: It glorifies intelligence and declares that willful ignorance is a bar to salvation.

Third: It holds sacred the free agency of man—

a. In giving to every individual the right to go to God,
b. In extending to its membership the encouragement to seek knowledge from all sources, and
c. By declaring that all things shall be done by common consent.

Fourth: It provides for progress—eternal progress— through continuous revelation, through the explanation of scientific discovery as a part of God's truth, through the adoption of what is superior though discovered by others. An instance: the adoption of the Scout system by the Church.

Fifth: It recognizes recreation as pleasing unto God. I believe we are the only people who have been not only permitted by authority, but commanded to re-create. It imposes implicit confidence in its young people. You may read the history of churches, but find if you can where the recreation has been turned over to the young people. It offers a field of ordinance activity that extends youthfulness into old age.

I sit in the Temple and I see more than a hundred people ready for the ordinances of that holy house. Here is a young couple to be married at the altar and I ask, "What visions are before them?" I see them full of youth—perfect youth. Youth in its full sense means physical strength, vigor, energy. Youth in its spiritual sense is measured by the faith, the hope, the love—there is love.

Beside this couple that are to be married for time and eternity that day, sits another couple. There is no physical youth there—perhaps three-score years have passed away, but they are to cause the wedding bells to ring in the spirit world at the end of that day and I have asked as I have looked into their faces and into the faces of the young couple, the one where the most physical youth is, "But in which couple is the most spiritual youth, the most faith, the most hope, the most love?" And I said, "There is youth brought back to old age and there is no old age in the midst of this ordinance which is characteristic alone of the Church I selected."

[George H. Brimhall, "The Church of My Choice," in *Long and Short Range Arrows,* comp. and ed. Harrison R. Merrill and Alice L. Reynolds, 2d ed. (Provo, Utah: Brigham Young University Press, 1936), 142–44.]

Eight "Ifs"

(Given as Parting Injunction to B. Y. U. Students—with apologies to Kipling)

1. If you can eat and drink to live and keep the stamp of wisdom on both work and play, you will possess the joys of health.
2. If you earn a little more than you expend and pay your debts of honor to your God and fellow men, you will be found among the well-to-do.
3. If you can enlarge some thought you have or get some new knowledge every day, you will be among the learned all your life.

4. If you can serve in such a way as to benefit yourself and others too, you will be among the honored of the earth.

5. If you can find one thing that others have not found or better than others yet have done it, you will stand somewhere upon the hill of fame.

6. If you can hold fast the friends you have and make new ones as you go, you will be happy.

7. If you can keep free from self-deception, doubt in God, and unfairness to your fellow men, you will be saved, today, tomorrow, and forever.

8. If you can remember and apply the things you in this school have learned, the other seven of these *If's* will fade away.

[George H. Brimhall, "Eight 'Ifs,'" in *Long and Short Range Arrows,* comp. and ed. Harrison R. Merrill and Alice L. Reynolds, 2d ed. (Provo, Utah: Brigham Young University Press, 1936), 198.]

Getting in Backward

On my recent trip to one of our stakes I discovered a person with notoriety. He was a community curiosity, a fellow who got into shows without paying for them by walking backwards when the doorkeeper was busy with the crowd. So well did he succeed that he boasted of his achievements.

The inevitable happened! He was watched and found a place prepared for him—a pivot chair, placed well to the front—a reserved seat. Just as the curtain rose the chair was swung round and our get-in-backward man found himself in a position fitting his method of getting in, his back to the stage and his face to the audience. And he was compelled to stay in as he got in.

This conduct, with its compensation, was not a refutation of the saying, "There is nothing new under the sun." Getting in backwards is all too common, too common in business—spending before we earn; too common in society—wanting good company without being willing to contribute a good individuality to society; in government—seeking position without preparation for it; in religion—by depending on doctrine without doing; in education—by dodging the daily grind.

The pleasure of getting in backward must be paid for by the chagrin of not being privileged to face the front, though we may get a front seat.

[George H. Brimhall, "Getting in Backward," in George H. Brimhall, *BYU Devotional Talks,* 2 vols. (n.p.: Alsina Elizabeth Brimhall Holbrook Family, 1988), 2:83]

Index

Page numbers in italics refer to graphics.

attendance of, 50

Brimhall's personal relationships with, 88–101

character of, 48–50, 53–58, 83, 84, 85–86, 94–101

different from pupils, 59–60

disciplining, 25–26, 56–57, 96–100

financial support for, 91–93

help finance new buildings, 139

loyalty of, 58

success of, 49–53

withdrawing from school, 83–84, 85, 99–100

Swensen, Russel B., 184–85

Swenson, John C., *169*

T

Talmage, James E., *89*

Tanner, Annie Clark, 171

teachers

issues facing, 71–72

training of, 58–61, 63–72, *69*

teaching. *See also* pedagogy

goals of, 48–51, 53, 59–60

Savior as role model for, 60

Temple Hill, 136, *137*, 137–38

testimony, 12, 28, 115, 133

Time magazine, *176*

Timpanogos Branch of the University of Deseret, xv, 13

U

University of Deseret, xv

V

Virgin River area, 5

W

Widtsoe, John A., 70

Wilkins, Alsina Elizabeth. *See* Brimhall, Alsina Elizabeth Wilkins (wife)

Wilkins, Catherine Augusta Lovett, 15

Wilkins, George Washington, 15

women, 71–72, 122, 134, 195

Women's Gymnasium, 144–45, *145*

Word of Wisdom, 49, 95, 101, 129, 141

World War I, 148–54

Y

Y Mountain, 134–36, *135*

Young, Brigham

considered education vital to Saints, xiv

counseled George W. Brimhall to marry, 2

prophesied of temple on Temple Hill, 137

wanted both sacred and secular teachings at BYA, xvi

Young Men's Academy (Spanish Fork), 14–15

Young Men's Mutual Improvement Association (YMMIA), 27–28, 29

Young Women's Mutual Improvement Association (YWMIA), 194